I0483198

Penetanguishene Ontario in Colour Photos, Saving Our History One Photo at a Time

Photography
by Barbara Raué
2016

Series Name: Cruising Ontario

Book 152: Penetanguishene

Cover photo: 83 Fox Street, Page

Series Name: Cruising Ontario
Saving Our History One Photo at a Time
in colour photos

Books Available in Alphabetical Order:
Aberfoyle, Acton, Alton, Amherstburg, Ancaster, Arthur, Aylmer, Ayr, Bloomingdale, Brantford, Burlington, Caledon, Caledonia, Cambridge, Clifford, Conestogo, Delhi, Dorchester to Aylmer, Drayton, Drumbo, Dundas, Eden Mills, Elmira, Elora, Essex, Fergus, Guelph, Hagersville, Hamilton, Hanover, Harriston, Hespeler, Jarvis, Kingston, Kingsville, Kitchener, Linwood, Listowel, London, Lucknow, Mono, Mount Forest, Neustadt, New Hamburg, Niagara-on-the-Lake, Oakville, Orangeville, Orillia, Owen Sound, Palmerston, Peterborough, Petrolia, Port Elgin, Preston, Rockwood, Sarnia, Seaforth, Sheffield, Shelburne, Simcoe, Southampton, St. Jacobs, St. Marys, St. Thomas, Stoney Creek, Stratford, Thamesford, Tillsonburg, Waterdown, Waterford, Waterloo, Welland, Wellesley, Windsor, Wingham, Woodstock

Book 123-124: Kingsville
Book 125-127: Woodstock
Book 128: Thamesford
Book 129-132: St. Marys
Book 133-136: Sarnia
Book 137: Petrolia
Book 138-139: Welland
Book 140-145: Kingston
Book 146-149: Ottawa
Book 150-151: Midland
Book 152: Penetanguishene

Other Books by Barbara Raue

Coins of Gold

Arrows, Indians and Love

The Life and Times of Barbara
Volume 1: Inventions That Have Enhanced My Life
Volume 2: Entertainment That I Have Enjoyed
Volume 3: East Coast Trips
Volume 4: Olympics Have Always Intrigued Me
Volume 5: Wonders of the World
Volume 6: Caribbean Cruises We Have Enjoyed
Volume 7: Animals
Volume 8: Storms and Other Major Disasters in My Lifetime
Volume 9: Wars, Terrorist Attacks and Major Disasters

The Cromwell Family Book

Laura Secord Discovered

Daddy Where Are You?

Montana Series
Book 1: Montana Dream
Book 2: Life on the Montana Frontier
Book 3: Montana to Boston and Back

Visit Barbara's website to view all of her books
http://barbararaue.ca

Table of Contents

Penetanguishene, sometimes shortened to Penetang, is a town on the southeasterly tip of Georgian Bay. It is a bilingual, French and English, community. The name means "land of the white rolling sands".

As early as 800 A.D., the Huron settled in semi-permanent villages in the area. The young French translator, Etienne Brule, was the first European to set foot in the Penetanguishene area between 1610 and 1614.

In 1793, John Graves Simcoe, the first Lieutenant Governor of Upper Canada, visited the area and saw the location's potential as a naval base. He wanted to use the bay to shelter warships to protect British interests on lakes Huron, Erie and Michigan. Beginning in 1814, the British-Canadians built the Penetanguishene Road to provide the area a land route to Barrie and Toronto, as it was previously accessible only by water transport along the rivers or across Georgian Bay. In 1828, the main British military establishment on the Upper Lakes moved from Drummond Island to Penetanguishene. Families of Metis fur traders who had moved with the British from Michilimackinac to Drummond Island after the War of 1812, moved again to Penetanguishene. The trip from Drummond Island took from fourteen to eighteen days and the bateaux were extremely crowded as they often carried eighteen people along with provisions and household goods. Although the naval base was closed in 1834, the military base remained until 1856. Some of the troops settled in the area after their service was complete providing an English-speaking population.

In the 1840s, French-speaking families from Quebec (mainly from the area immediately east of Montreal), attracted by promises of cheap and fertile land, joined the French-speaking settlers already in the area. Later, as the logging industry began to develop, more English-speaking settlers arrived. Penetanguishene became the local market and meeting place for these individuals. Many of Penetanguishene's families today are descended from the Québécois settlers who arrived in the 1800s.

Alfred Andrew Thompson came to Penetanguishene in 1830 at the age of 15 to work as an assistant to Andrew Mitchell, Sr., a fur trader on Water Street. In 1840, Alfred erected a mercantile store on the corner of Water and Main Streets known as the Green Block. It was the only market in the area where farmers could sell their produce of butter, eggs, and vegetables for cash to pay their taxes. In 1847, Alfred married Sarah Anne Burke and they had three sons and two daughters. Alfred was an Anglican involved in the affairs of St. James-on-the-Line Church.

Michael Gendron, born in Quebec of French parents, came here in 1835 and established a tannery on the banks of Copeland's Creek, and later a second tannery on Main Street. "Gendron Penetangs" were a type of moccasin made of hand-stretched, oil-tanned leather, sturdy enough to be used by lumberjacks, prospectors, hunters and surveyors. They were regulation issue for soldiers in World War I.

Joseph Dubeau and his family came to the area in 1859; he started a livery stable and moved families from Penetanguishene to Midland.

The C. Beck Manufacturing Company operated from 1875 to 1969 selling wholesale lumber, shingles, lath, pails, tubs and woodenware to firms in Ontario, Quebec, western Canada and the northern United States.

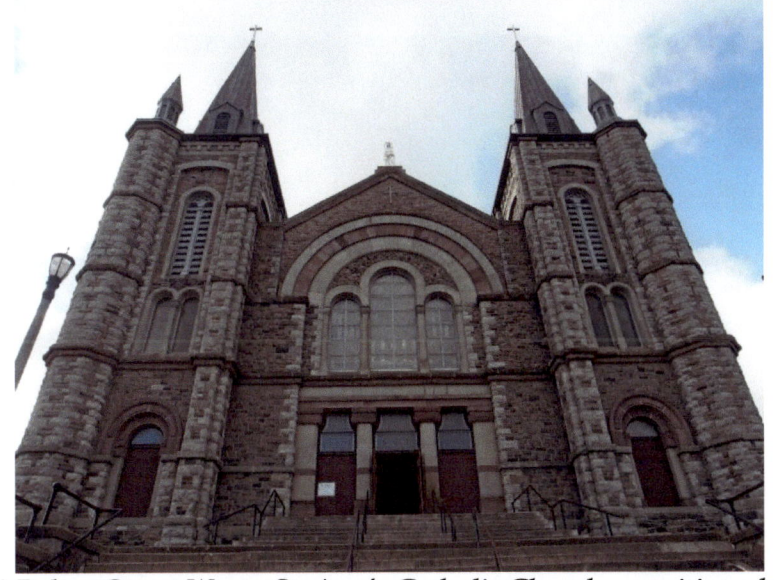

28 Robert Street West - St. Ann's Catholic Church – positioned to
overlook the town and the bay – constructed with limestone
between 1886 and 1902; it serves a bilingual Catholic community
with services held in French and English – Romanesque style

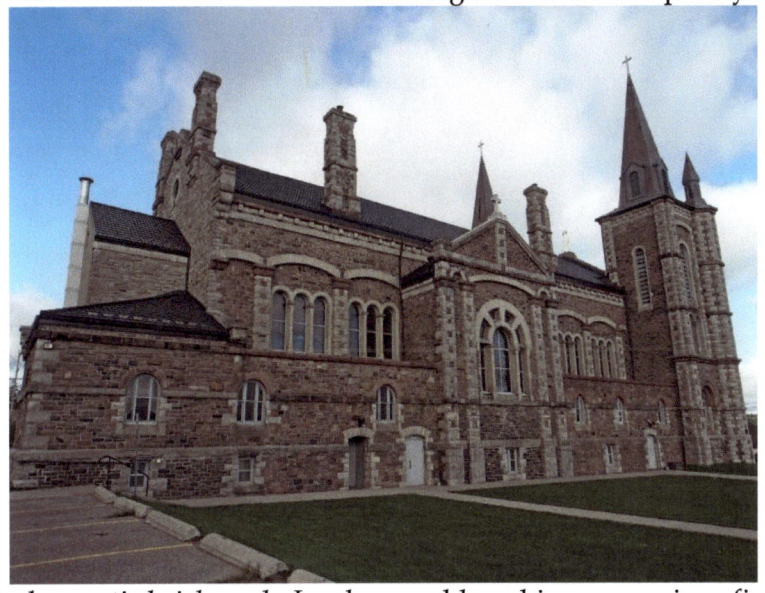

Polychromatic brickwork, Jacobean gables, chimneys, spires, finials

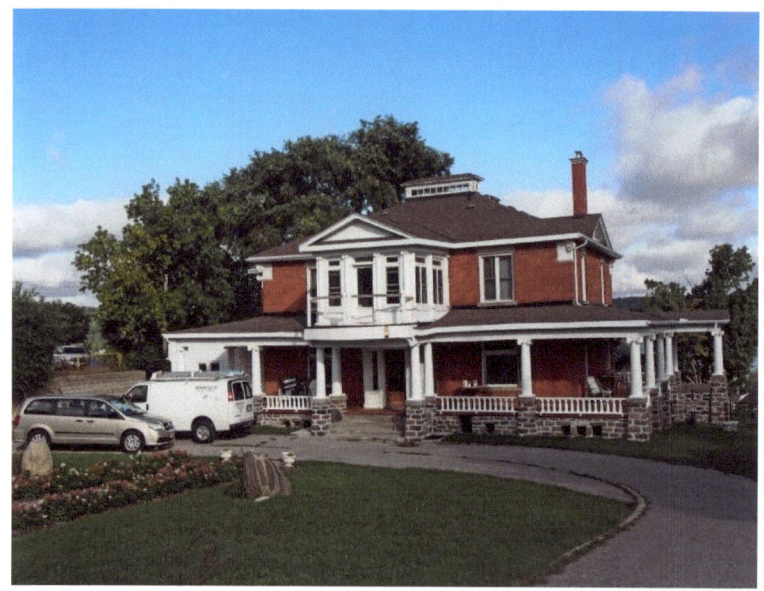

33 Robert Street – J. T. Payette's home (ran P. Payette Foundry – machine shop; built many mills)

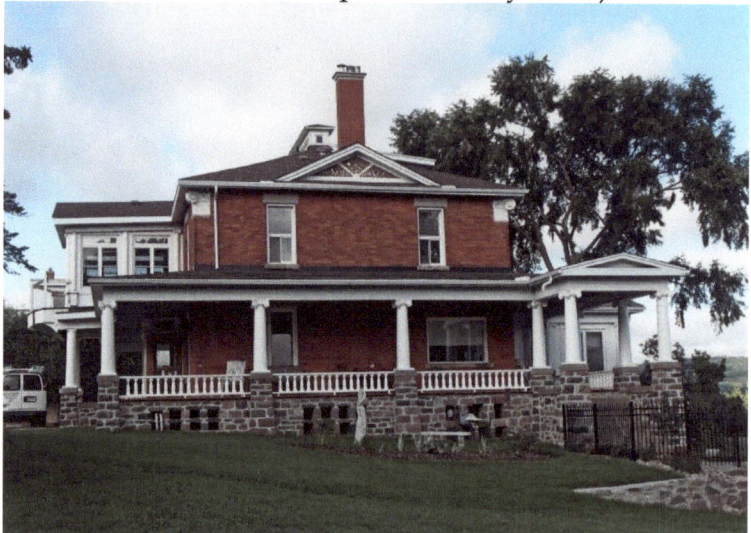

Cobblestone foundation, Ionic pillars, belvedere, open railings, pediments, sidelights

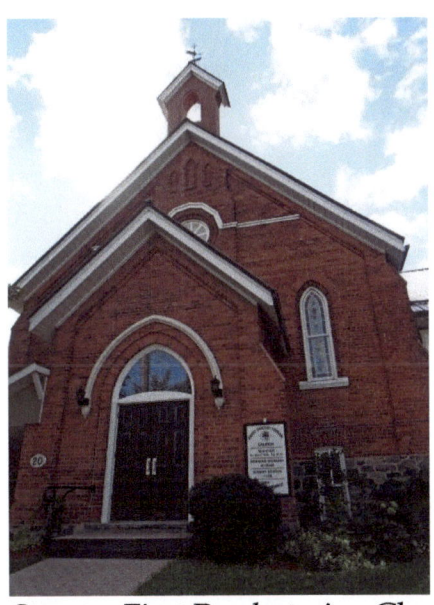

20 Robert Street – First Presbyterian Church - 1887
Buttresses, lancet and stained glass windows, cupola, rose window

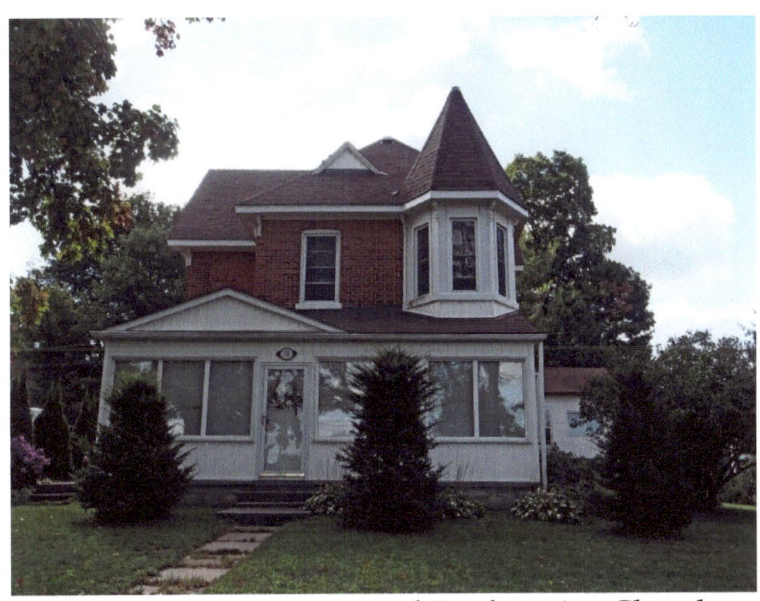

18 Robert Street – turret – original Presbyterian Church manse

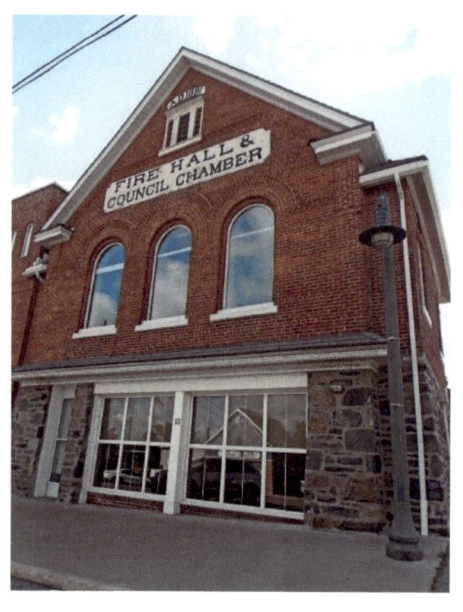

10 Robert Street – Fire Hall and Council Chamber - 1891

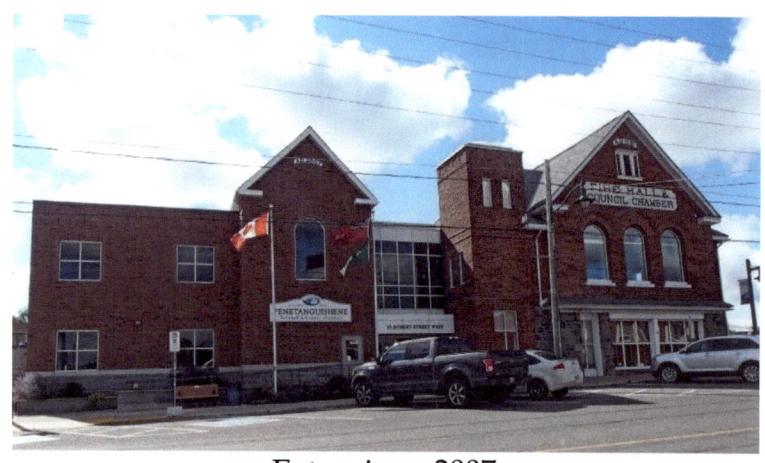

Extension - 2007

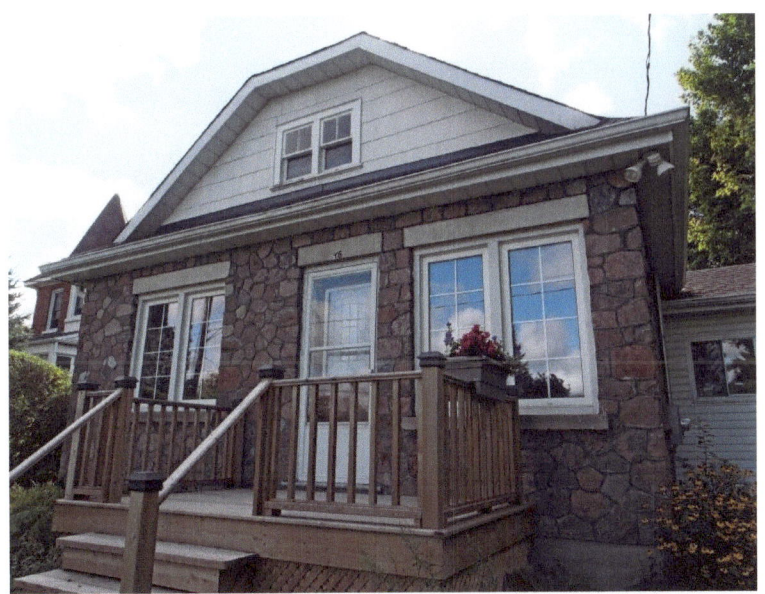

16 Robert Street

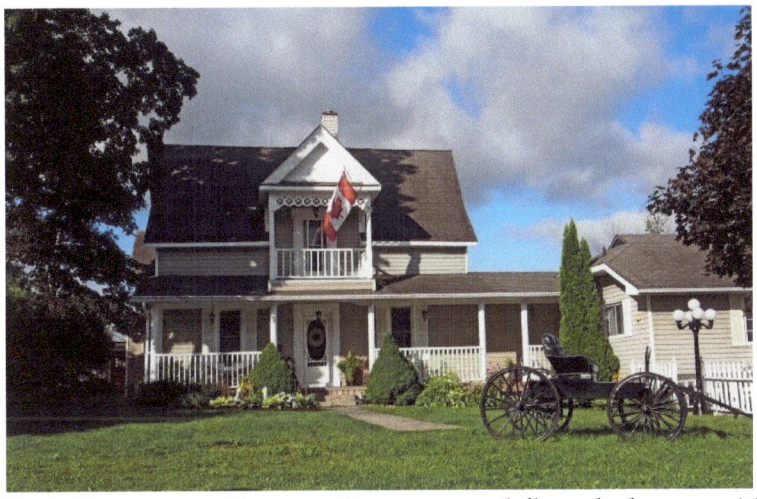

Owen Street – pediment above second floor balcony with open railing, and decorative trim at top of square piers, round-pillared verandah with open railing

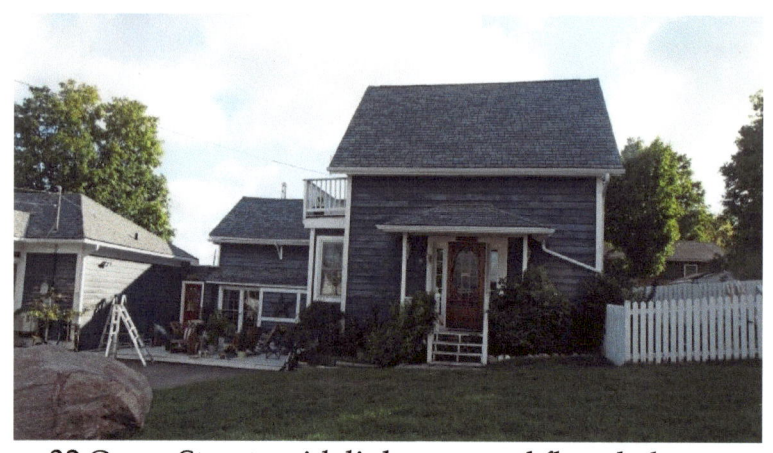

32 Owen Street – sidelights, second floor balcony

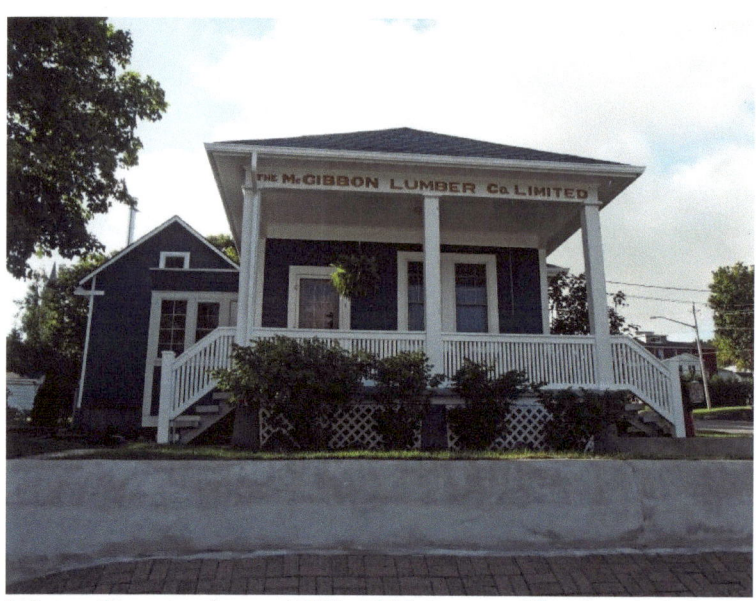

32 Water Street – from 1878-1882 it was Charlwood Grocery operated by merchant Mr. Dodge; in 1882 David Davidson used it as an office for his lumber company; between 1905 and 1910 the McGibbons bought out Davidson and it became the McGibbon Lumber Company office

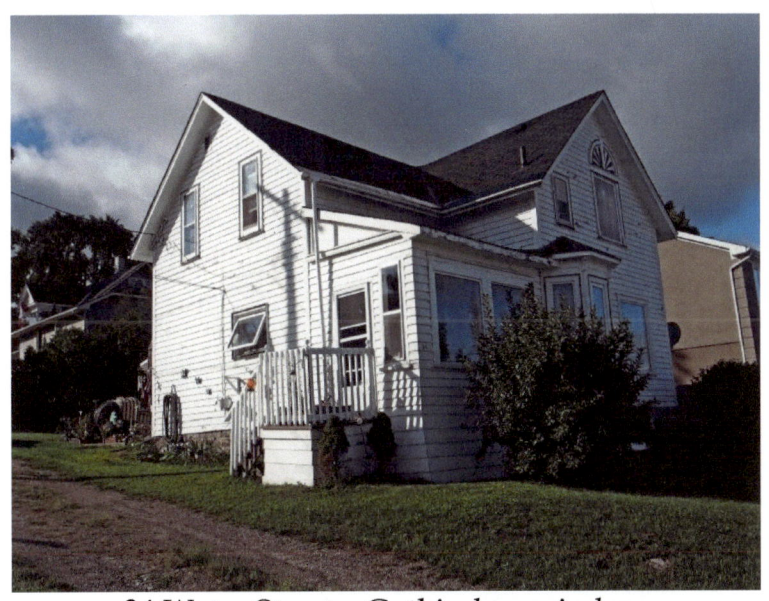

34 Water Street – Gothic, bay window

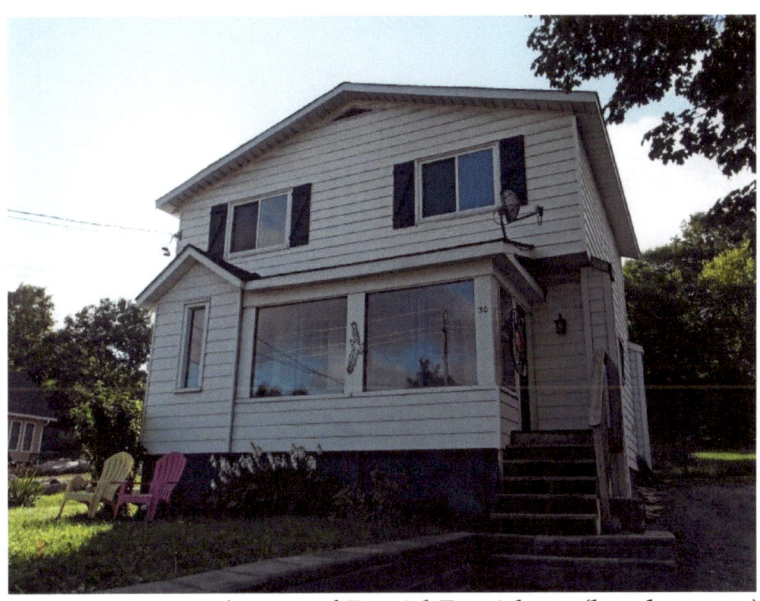

30 Water Street – home of David Davidson (lumberman) –
1879

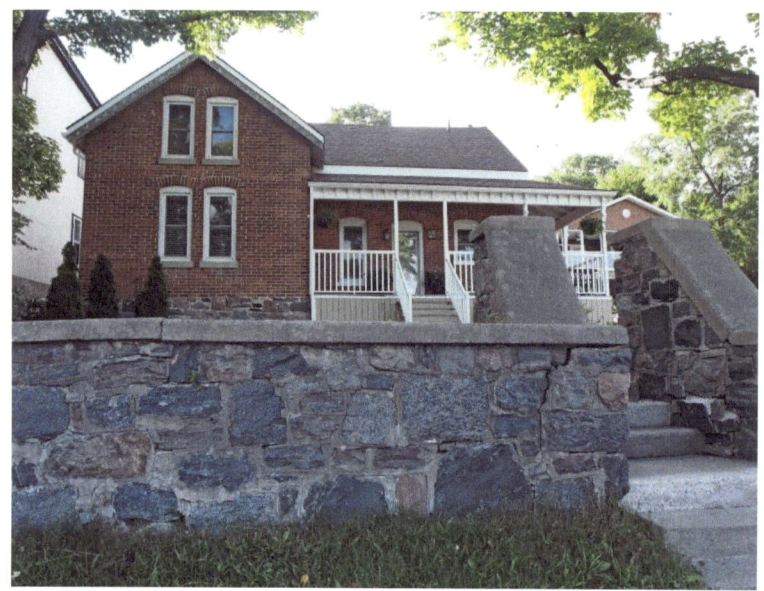

26 Water Street – 1877 – C. E. Wright's flour and feed store
Gothic – voussoirs over windows

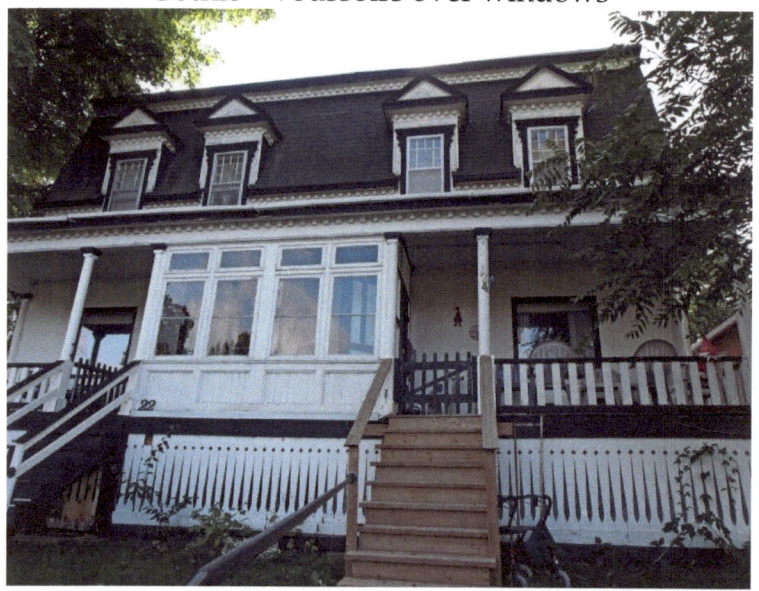

22 Water Street; 24 Water Street – 1881 – James Smith Home
Dormers in Mansard roof, open railing on verandah

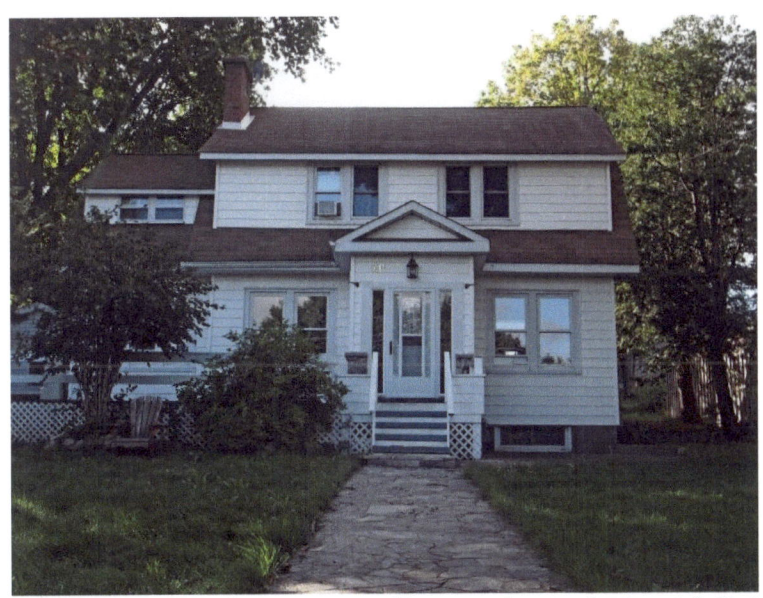

20 Water Street – dormers, pediment above door, sidelights

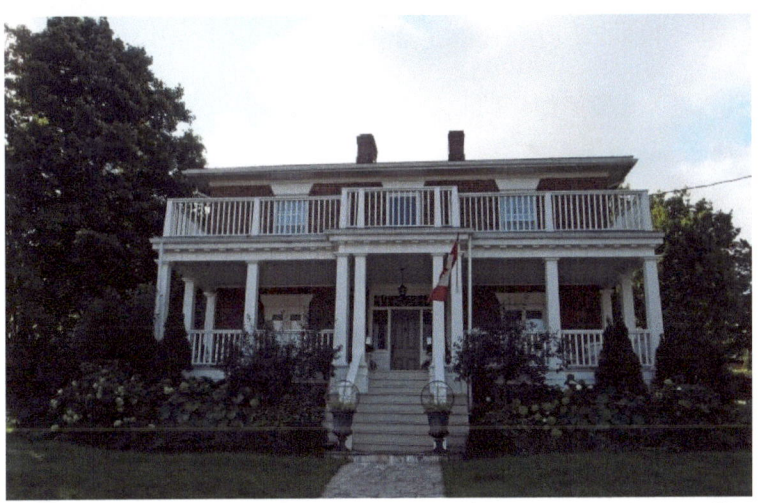

14 Water Street – Alfred Andrew Thompson House (first mayor – he married Sara-Anne Burke; he built the Green Block at 1 Water Street) – 1882 – brick house two-storey verandah, open railing, sidelights and transom

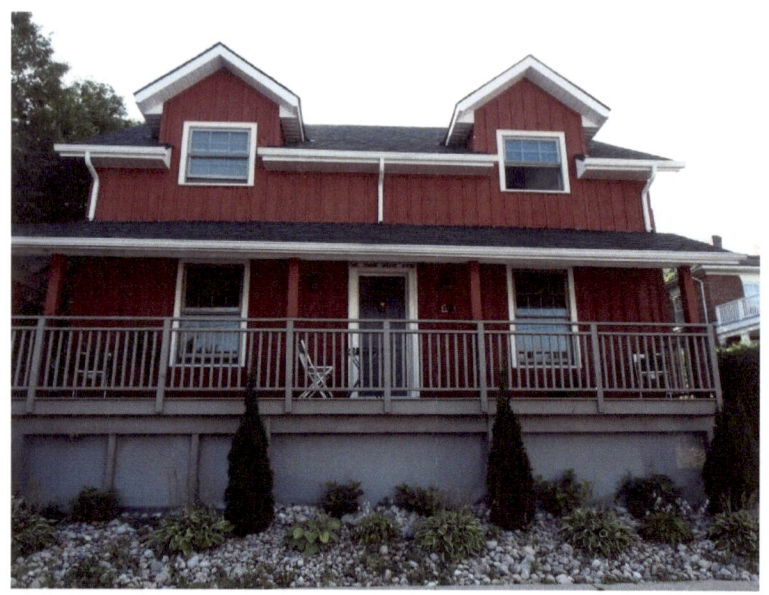

12 Water Street – Robert Gordon House – 1828 – Robert Gordon came from the British Garrison at Drummond Island – cedar log house, dormers, open railing

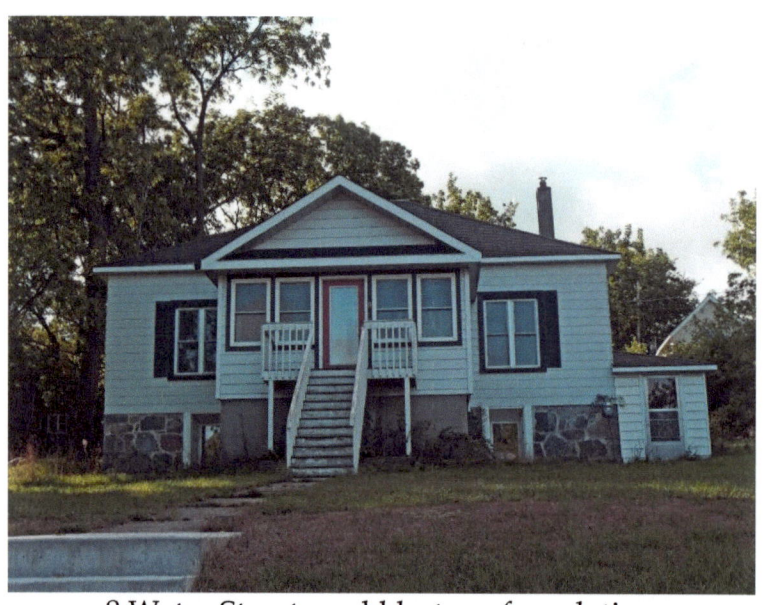

8 Water Street – cobblestone foundation

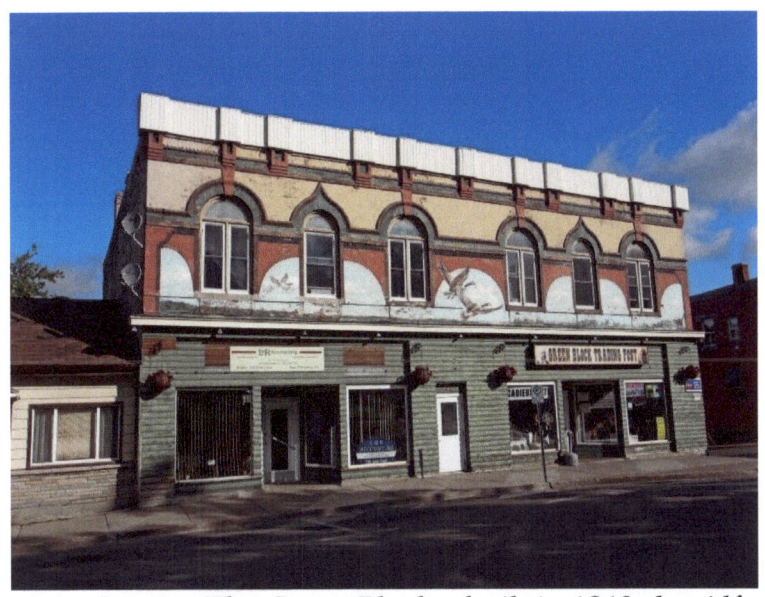

1 Water Street – The Green Block – built in 1840s by Alfred Andrew Thompson (he painted it green) for his mercantile business – now called Green Block Trading Post – voussoirs, keystones, Canada Geese mural

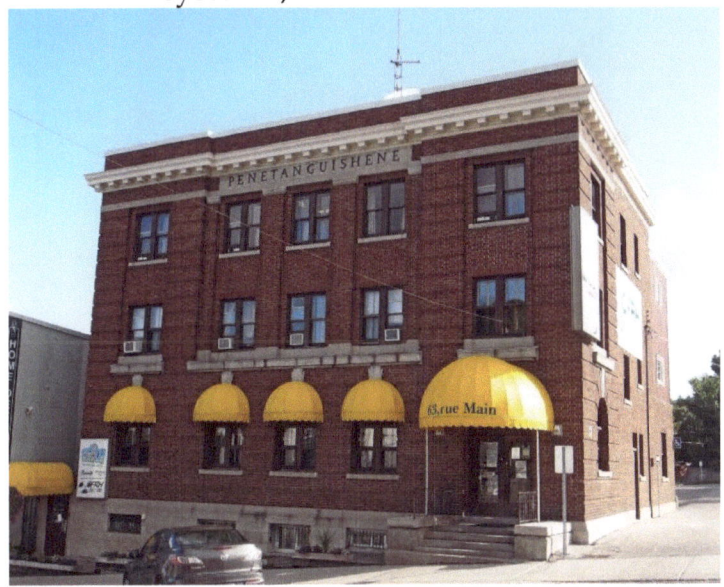

63 Main Street – 1934 – Post Office – voussoirs, keystones on first floor windows, decorative cornice trim

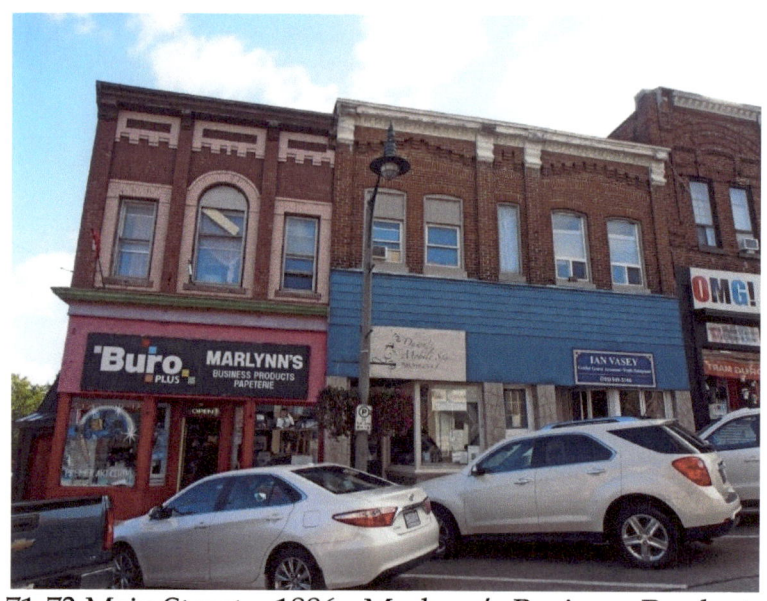

71-73 Main Street – 1886 - Marlynn's Business Products
Dentil moulding, pilasters

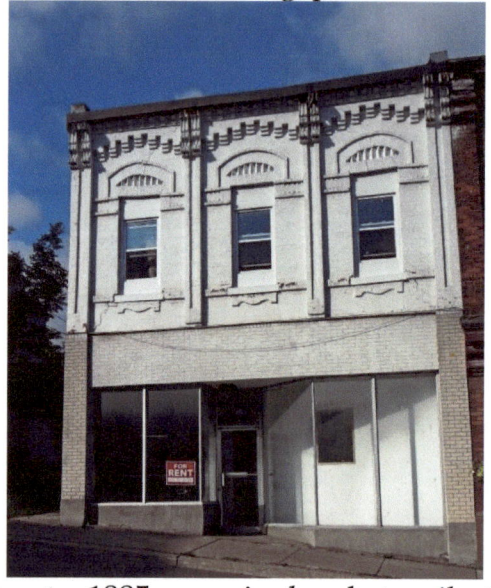

78 Main Street – 1885 – cornice brackets, pilasters, dentil
moulding, saw tooth brickwork

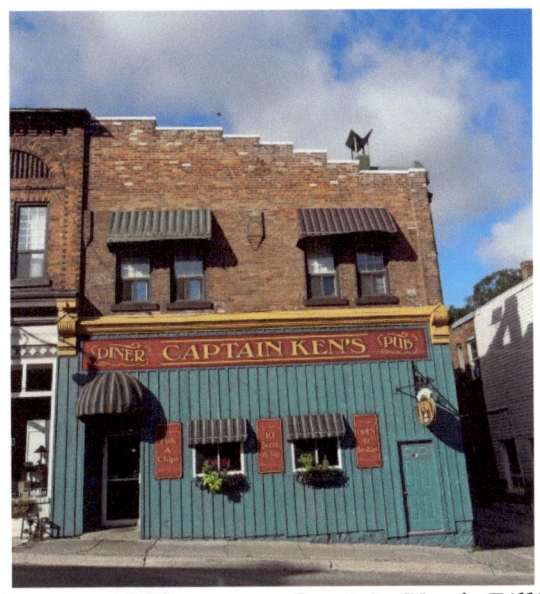

70 Main Street – 1890s – now Captain Ken's Billiards and Restaurant – decorative brickwork across width of second storey, stepped roofline

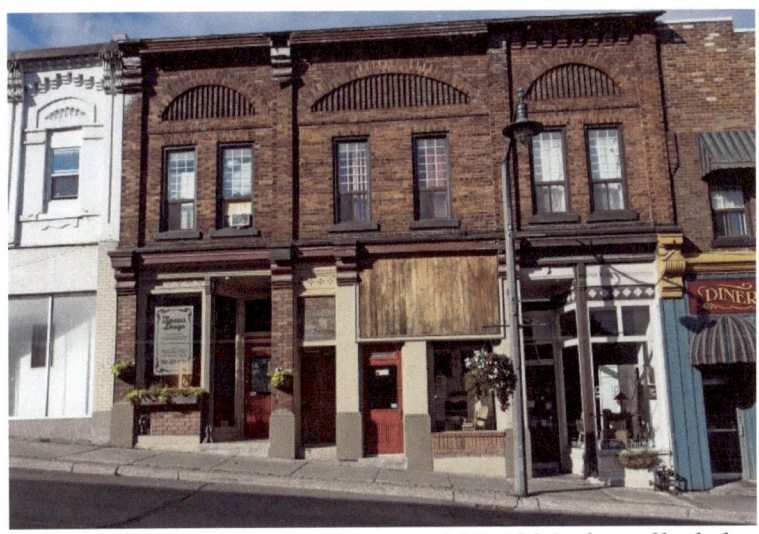

74-76 Main Street – Beck Block – 1885-1886 - bevelled dentil moulding, decorative brickwork (saw tooth arrangement of bricks), pilasters

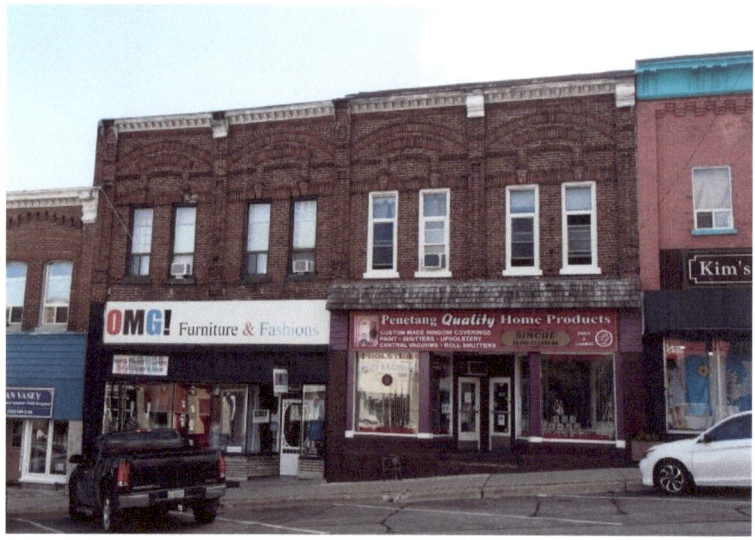

77-81 Main Street – OMG Furniture, Quality Home Products
Decorative brickwork, pilasters, voussoirs, keystones

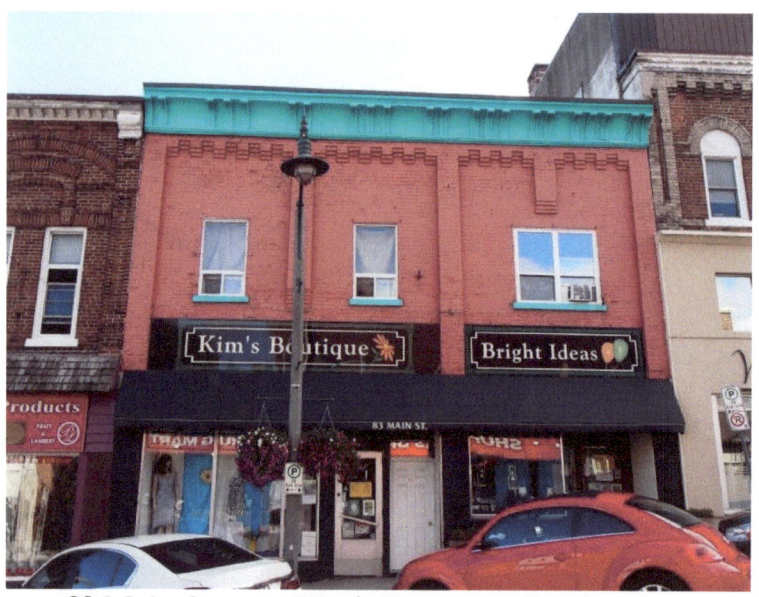

83 Main Street – Kim's Boutique, Bright Ideas
Pilasters, bevelled dentil moulding

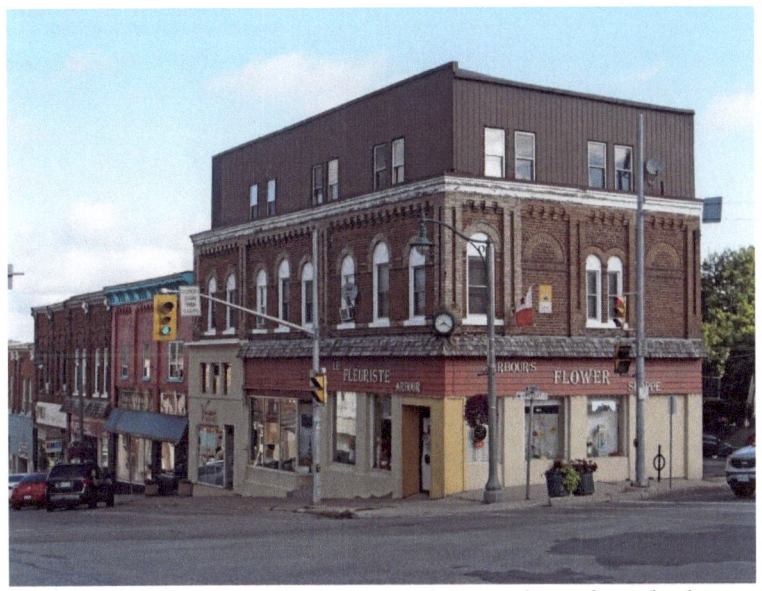

89 Main Street – used to have a Mansard roof with dormers
Bevelled dentil moulding, pilasters, voussoirs, dichromatic
brick work

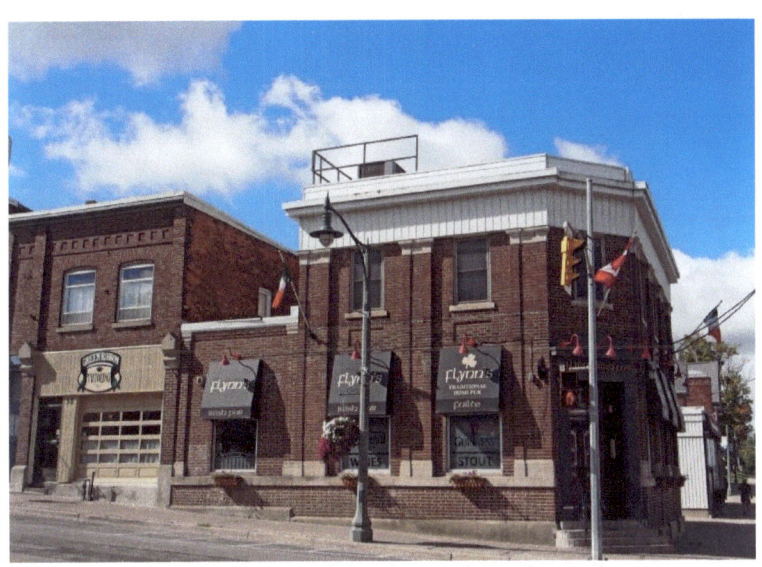

96 Main Street – Flynn's Irish Pub - pilasters

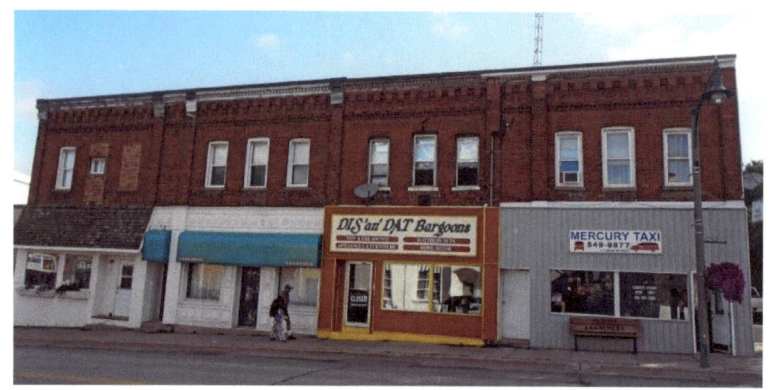

111 Main Street – Dis 'an' Dat Bargoons - dentil and bevelled moulding, pilasters

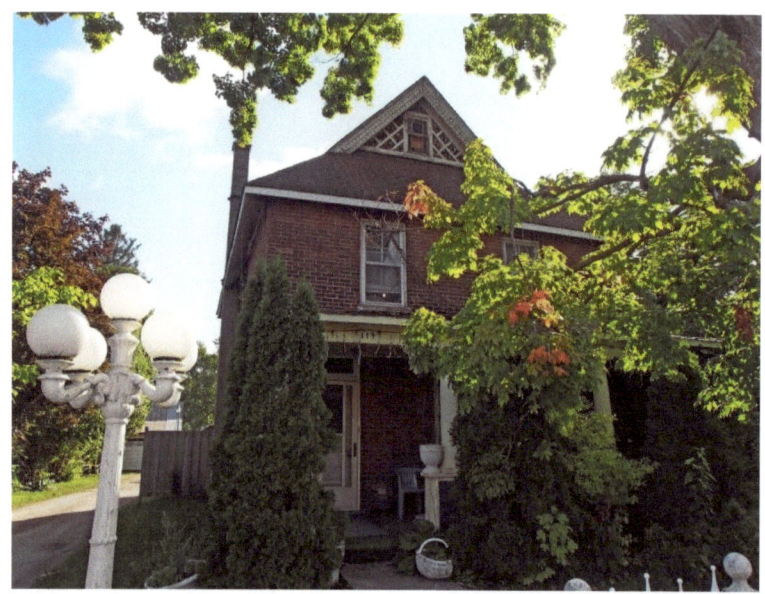

119 Main Street – gable dormer with decorative verge board

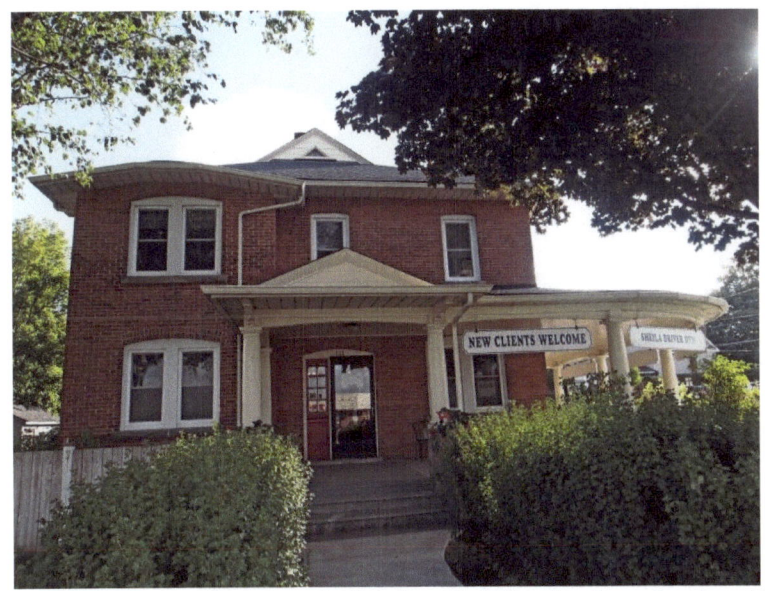

131 Main Street – home of Charles E. Wright (butcher) – 1912

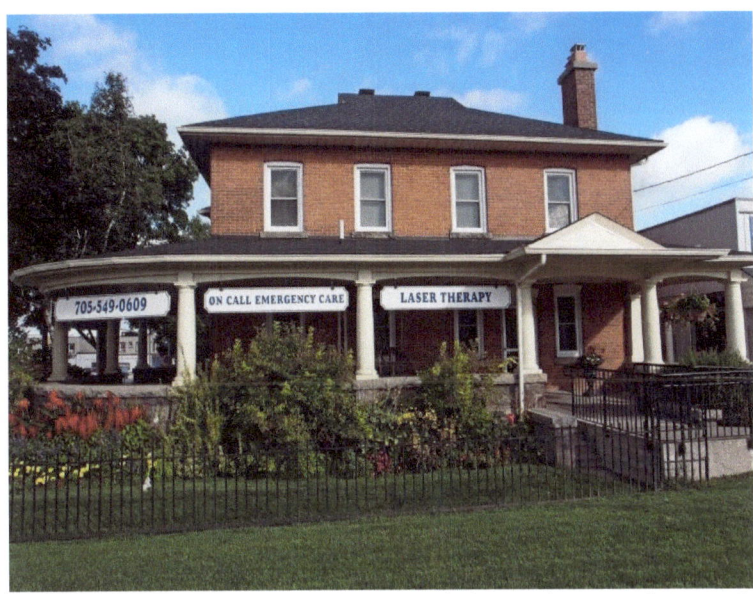

Doric pillars on wraparound verandah, pediment, hipped roof

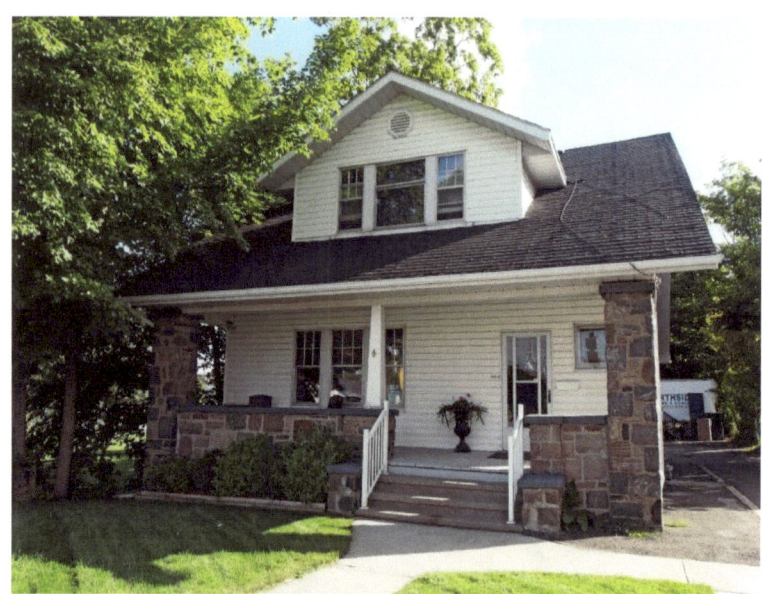

129 Main Street – cobblestone verandah piers and closed railing, large dormer

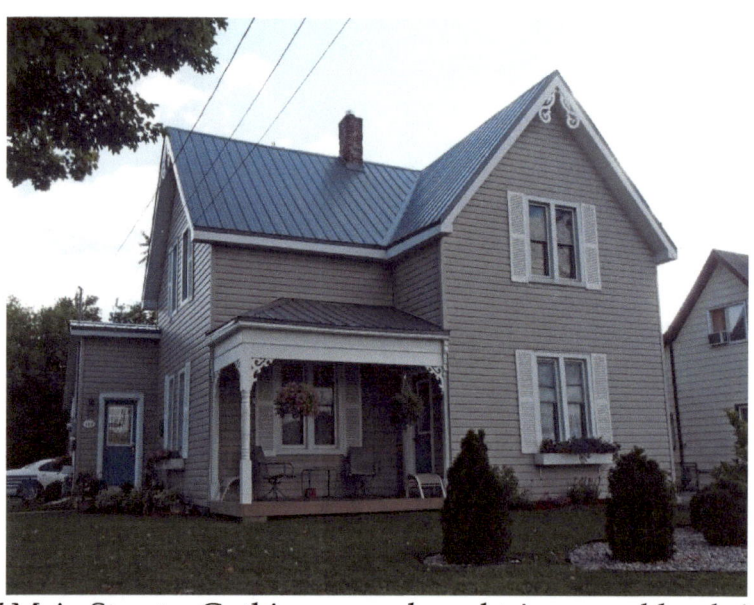

147 Main Street – Gothic – verge board trim on gables, bric-a-brac at top of turned wood verandah supports

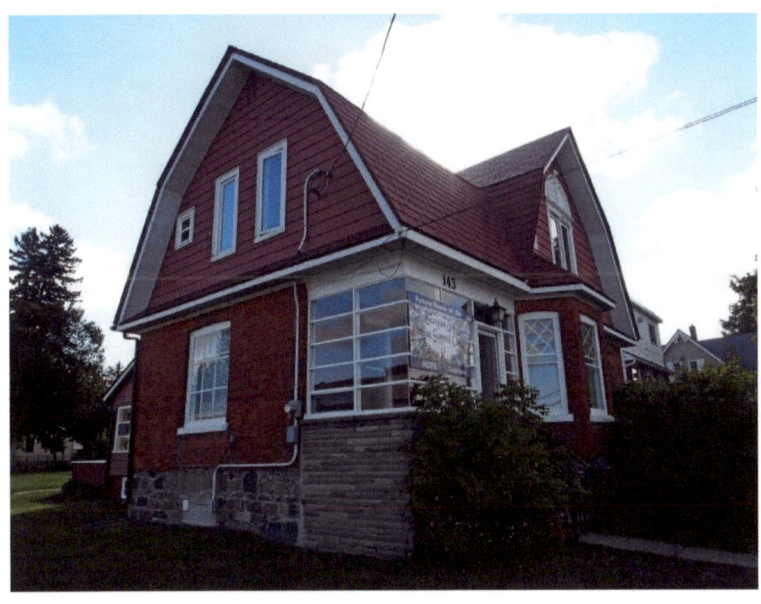

143 Main Street – Gambrel roof, Neo-colonial style

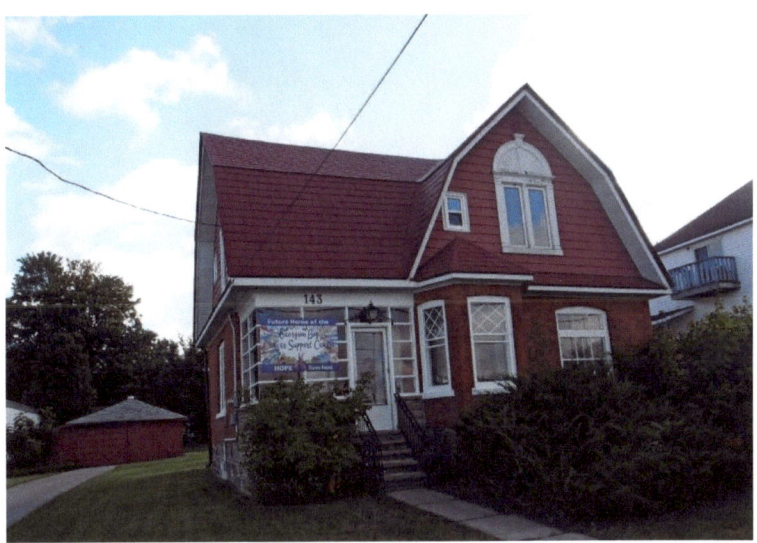

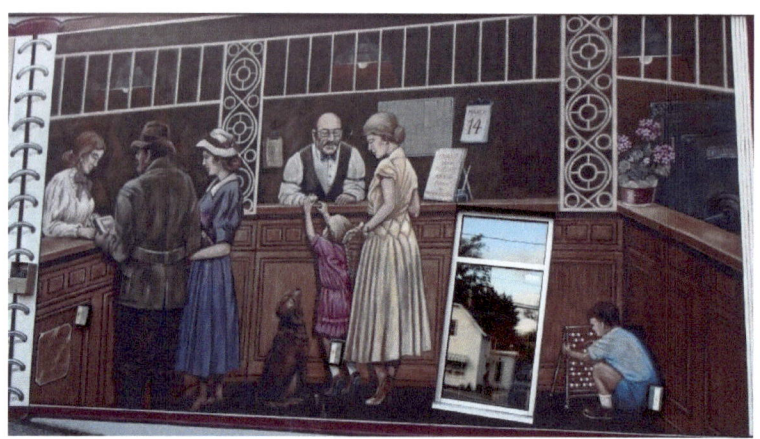

Mural - Bank of Nova Scotia – 1832 – Penetang branch opened in 1956

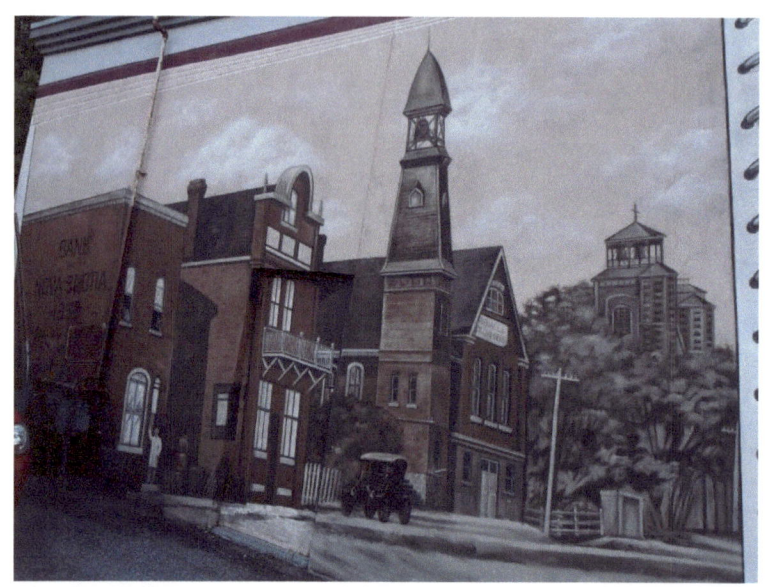

Mural - Robert Street – Old Town Hall, St. Ann's Church

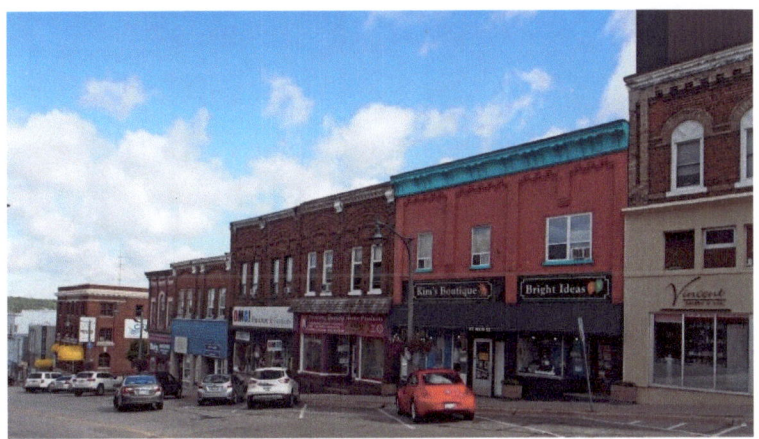

Main Street

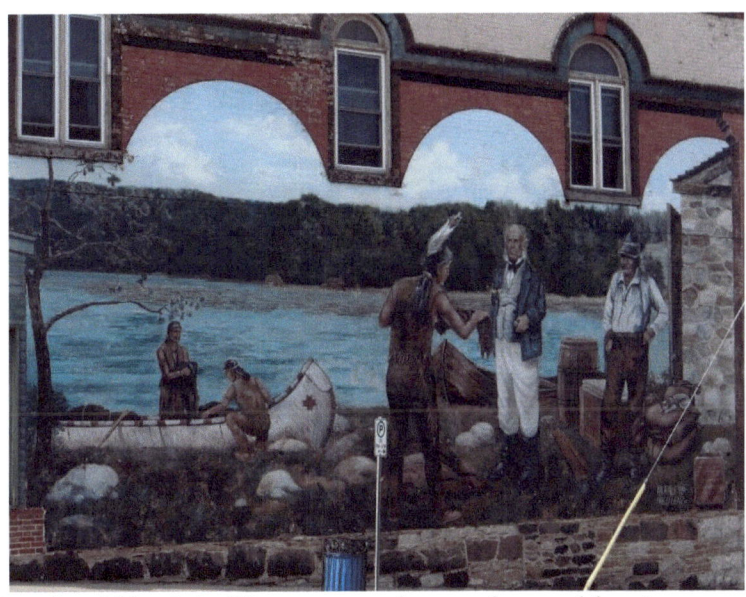

Mural – Alfred A. Thompson, fur trader and businessman,
first mayor of Penetanguishene in 1882

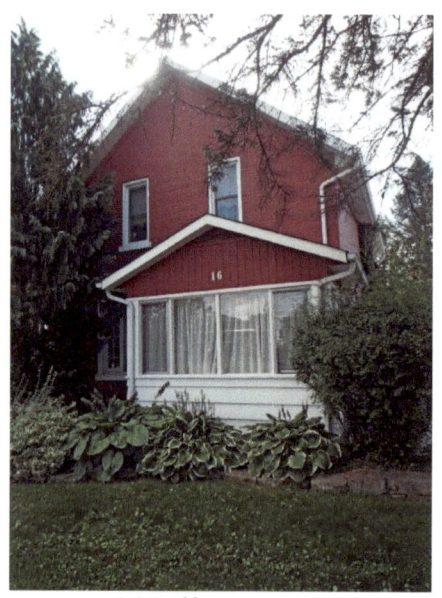

16 Jeffery Street

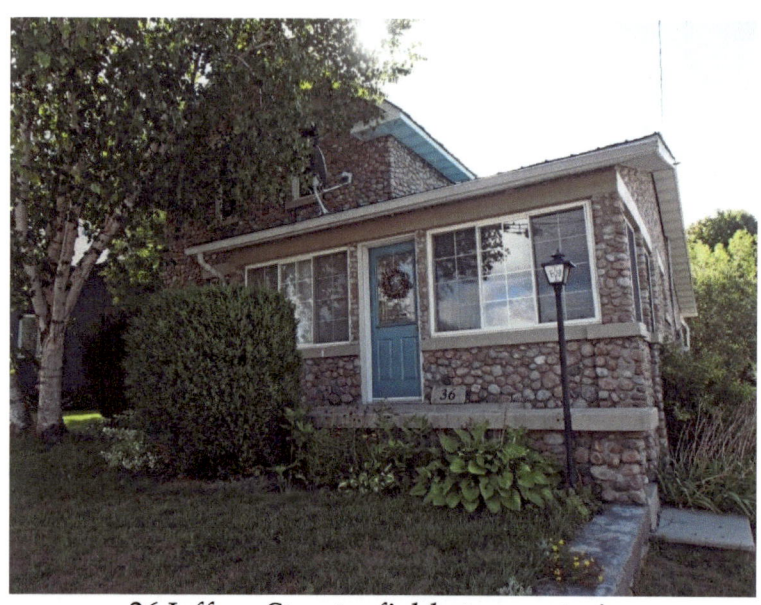

36 Jeffery Street – field stone exterior

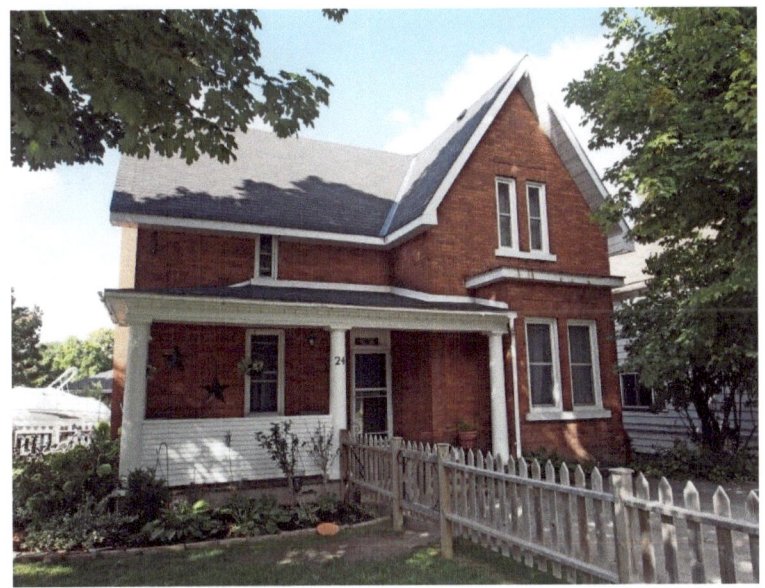

24 Harriet Street – Gothic – Doric pillars as veranda supports

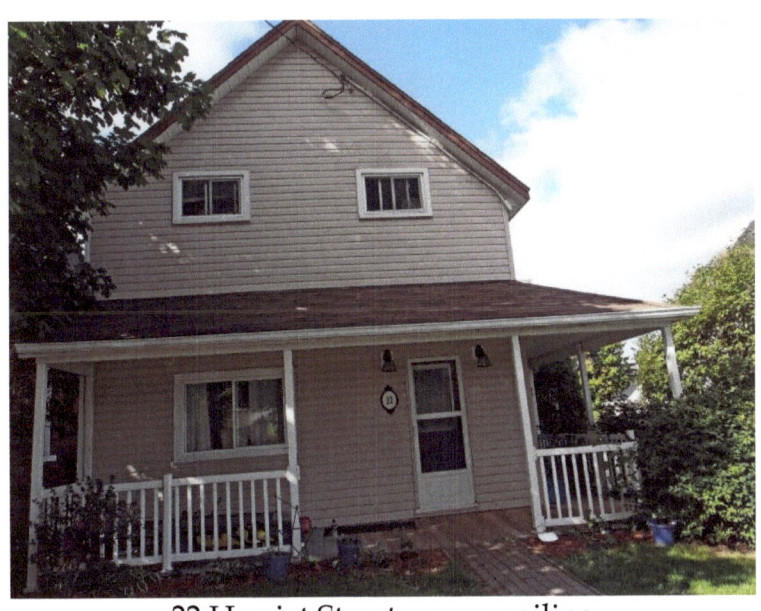

22 Harriet Street – open railing

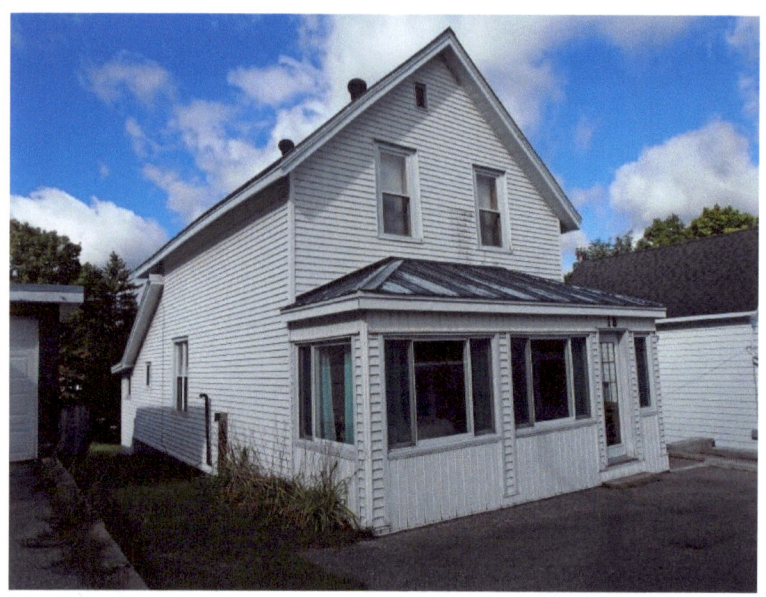

18 Harriet Street – Gothic with saltbox rear section, enclosed porch

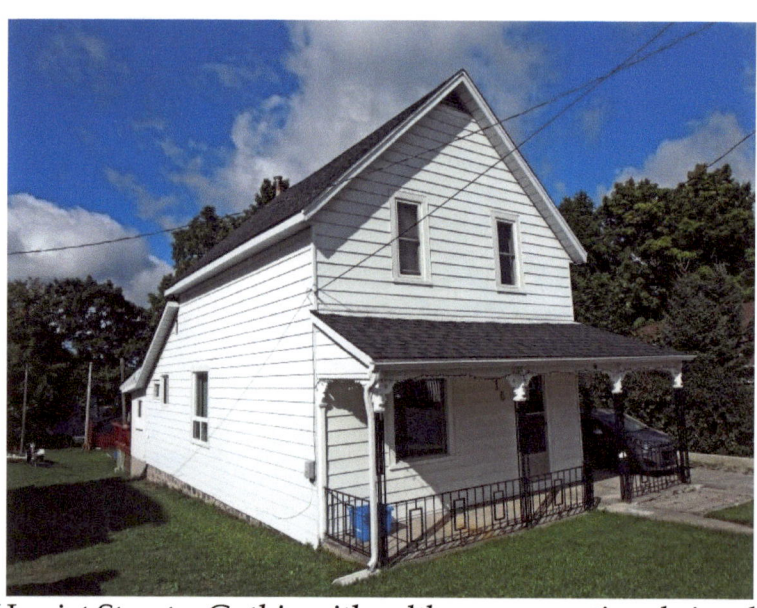

16 Harriet Street – Gothic with saltbox rear section, bric-a-brac at top of verandah supports, open railing

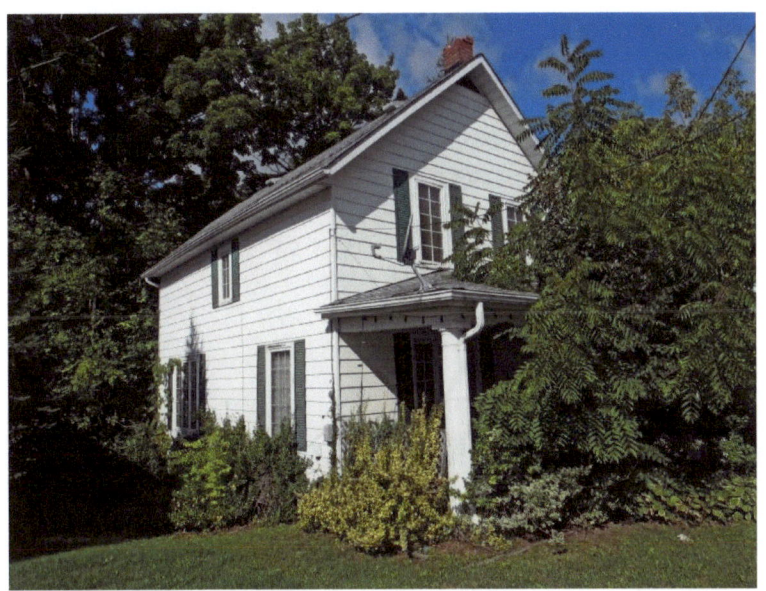

Harriet Street – Gothic – Doric pillars on veranda

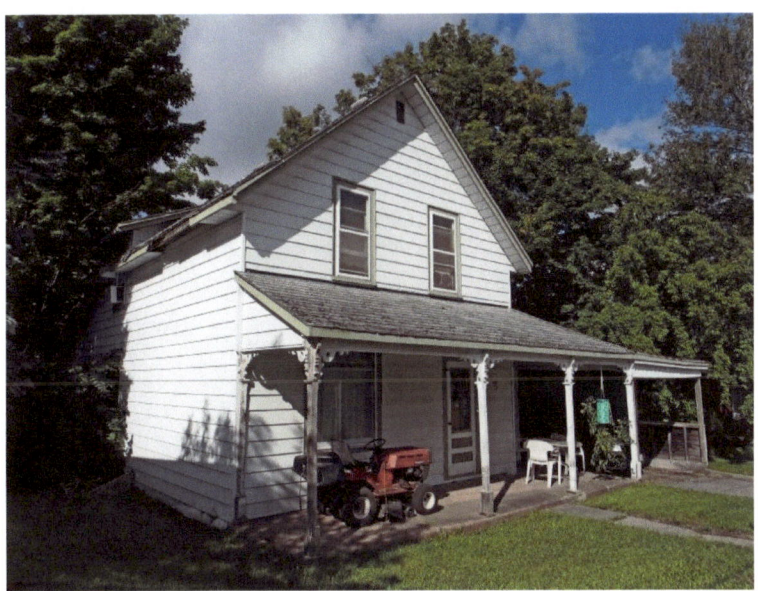

8 Harriet Street – Gothic - bric-a-brac at top of verandah supports

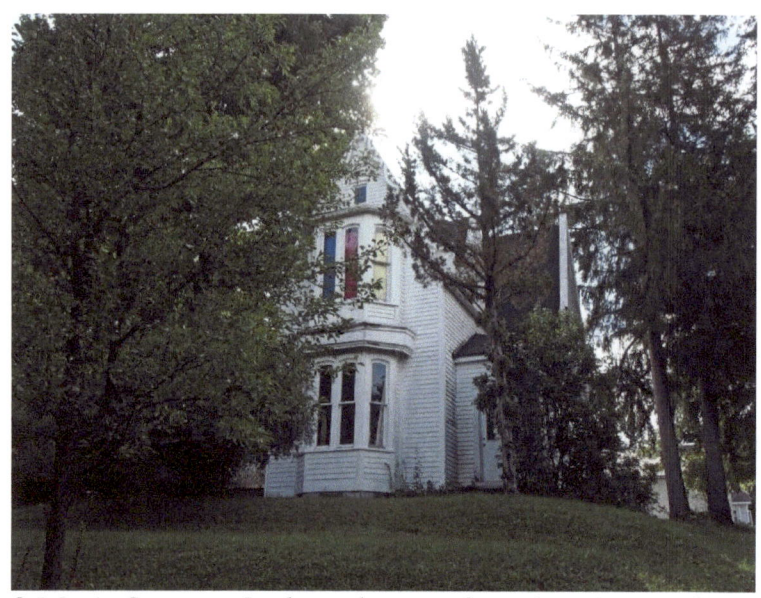

3 Maria Street – Gothic – home of Frederick W. Jeffery (bookkeeper) – 1878 – steeply pitched gable roof, verge board trim on gables, two-storey bay window, dormer

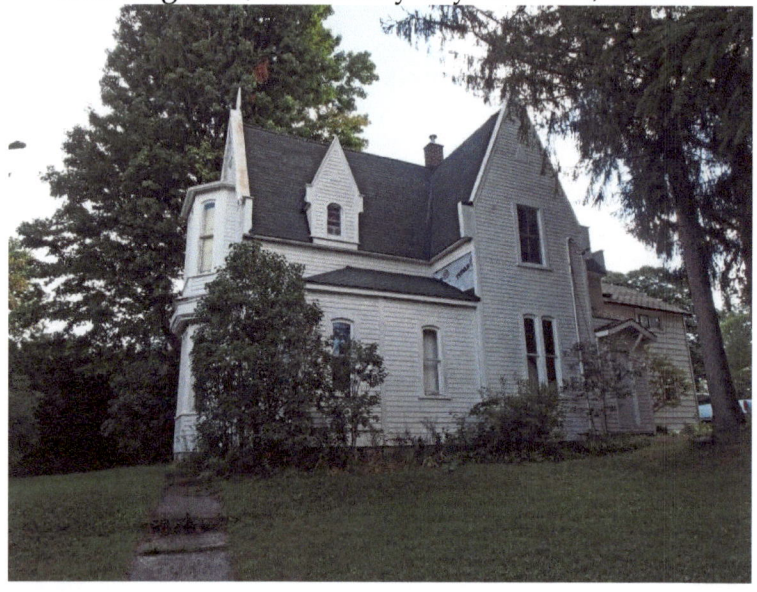

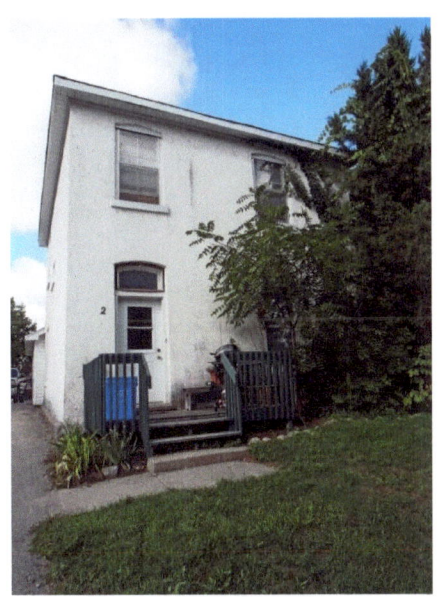

2 Maria Street

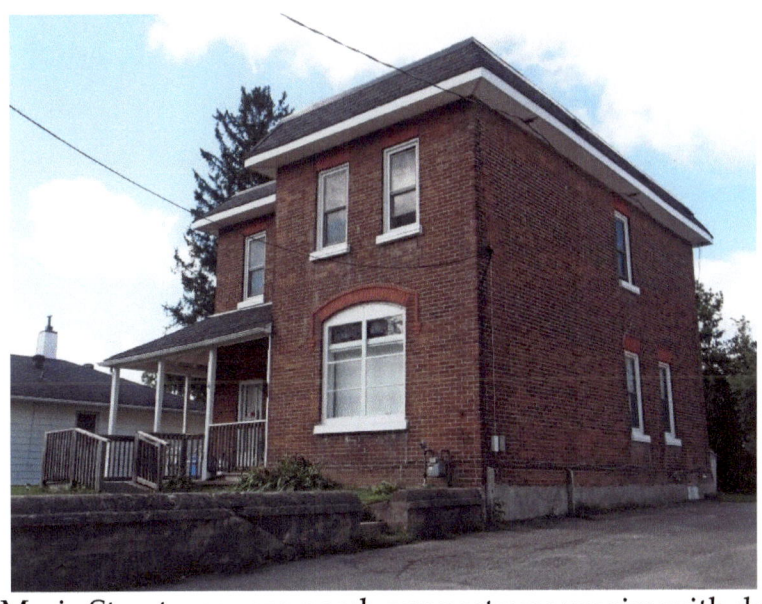

4 Maria Street – square porch supports; voussoirs with drip molds

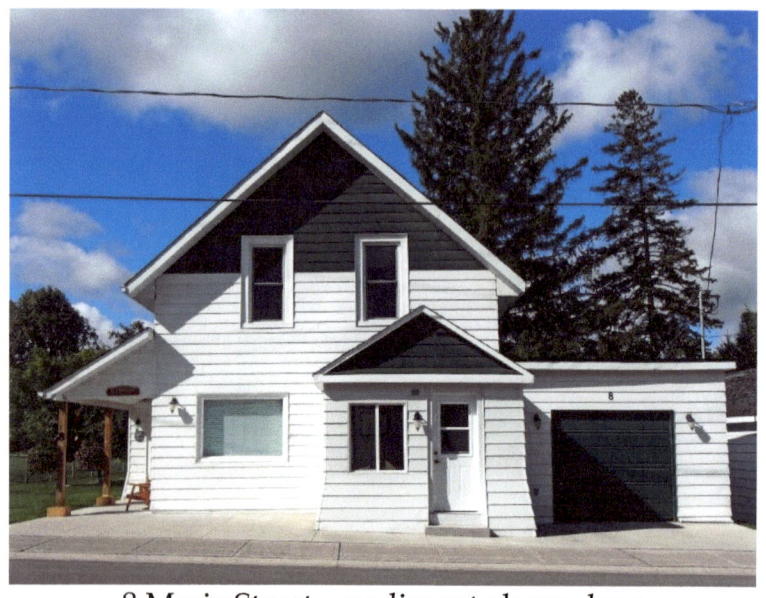

8 Maria Street – pediment above door

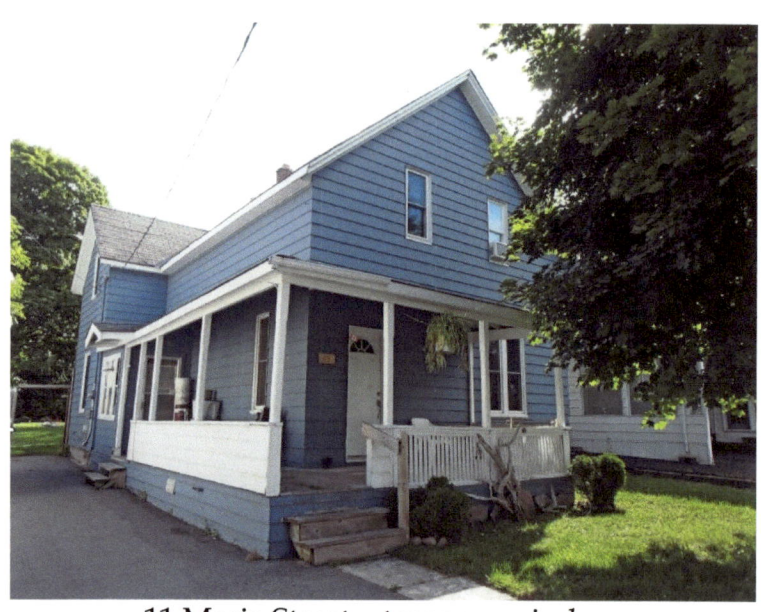

11 Maria Street – transom window

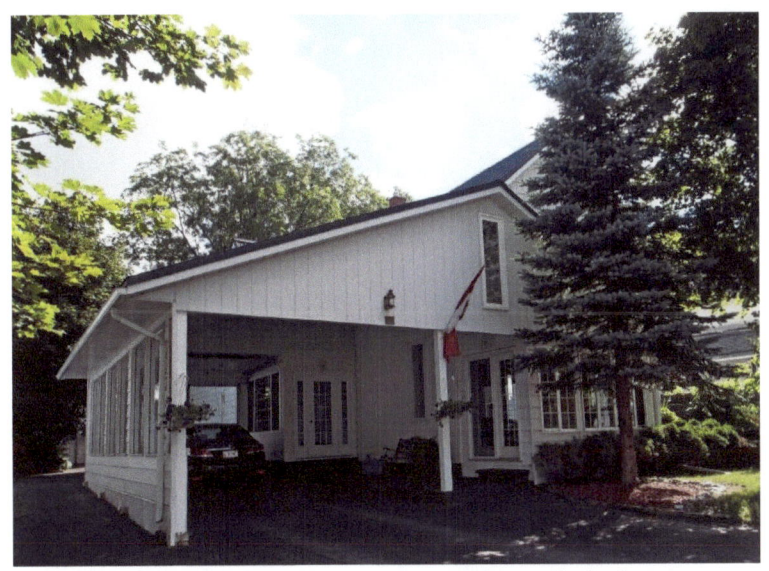

13 Maria Street – vernacular - sidelights

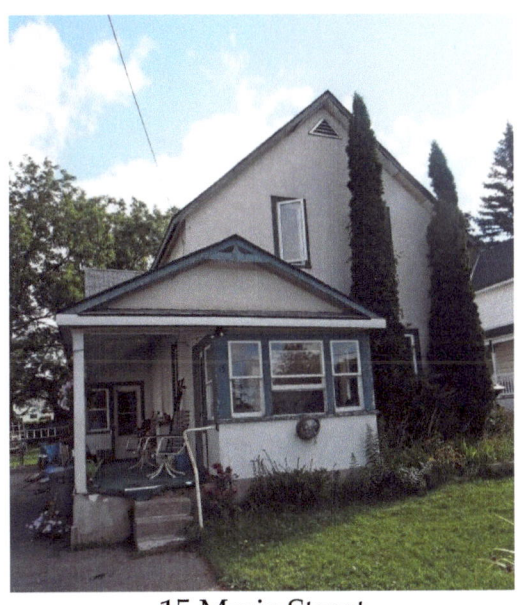

15 Maria Street

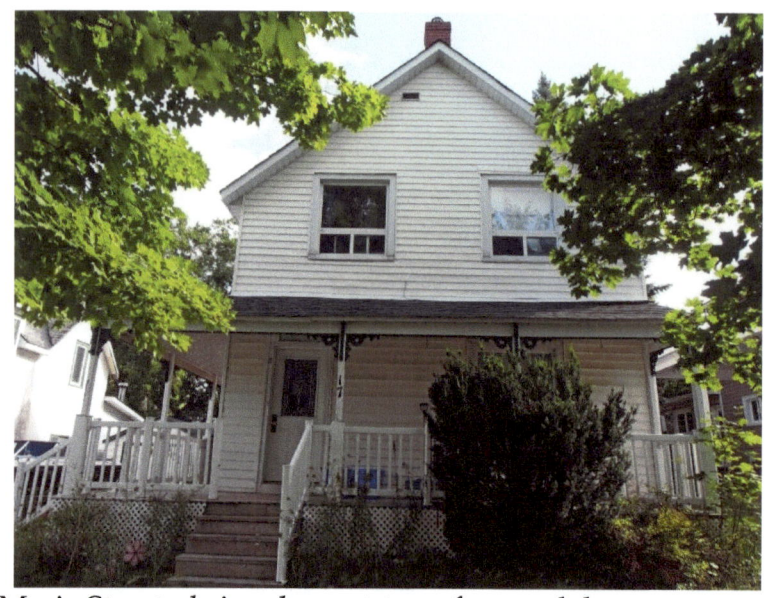

17 Maria Street - bric-a-brac at top of verandah supports, open railing

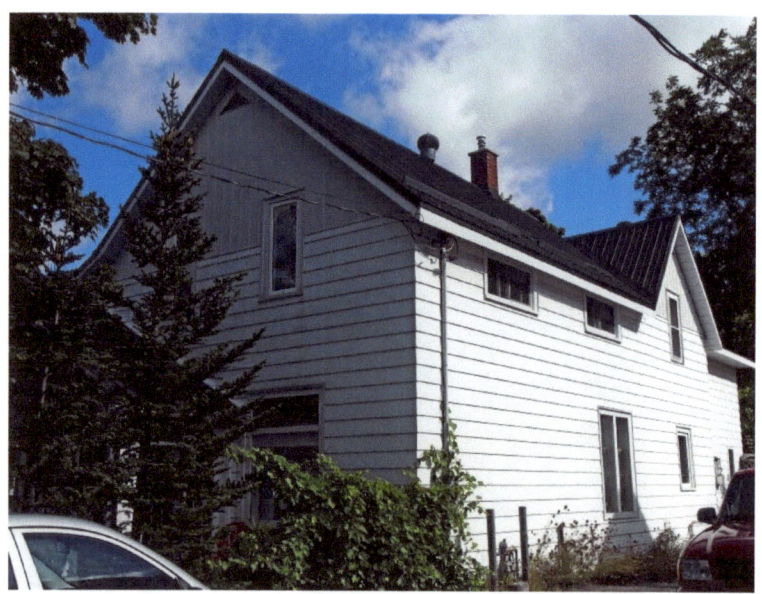

Maria Street – Gothic – clapboard siding

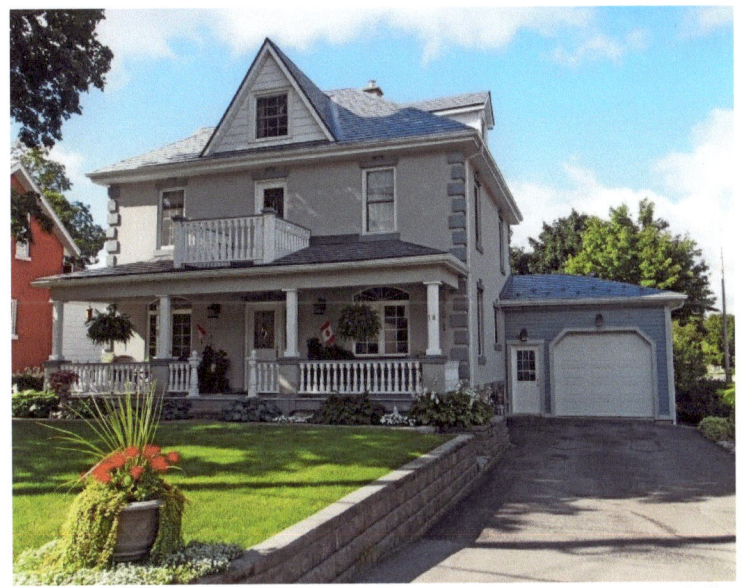

18 Maria Street – hipped roof with dormers, second floor balcony, corner quoins, multi-paned transom windows above large first storey windows, open spindle railing

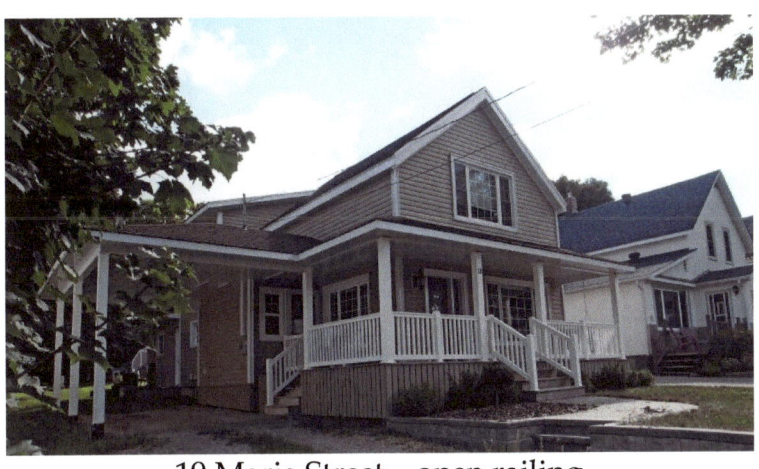

19 Maria Street – open railing

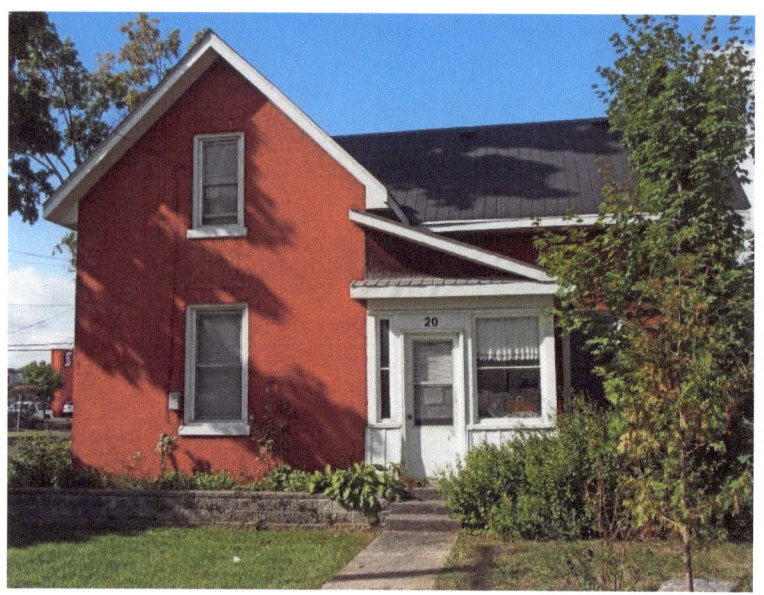

20 Maria Street

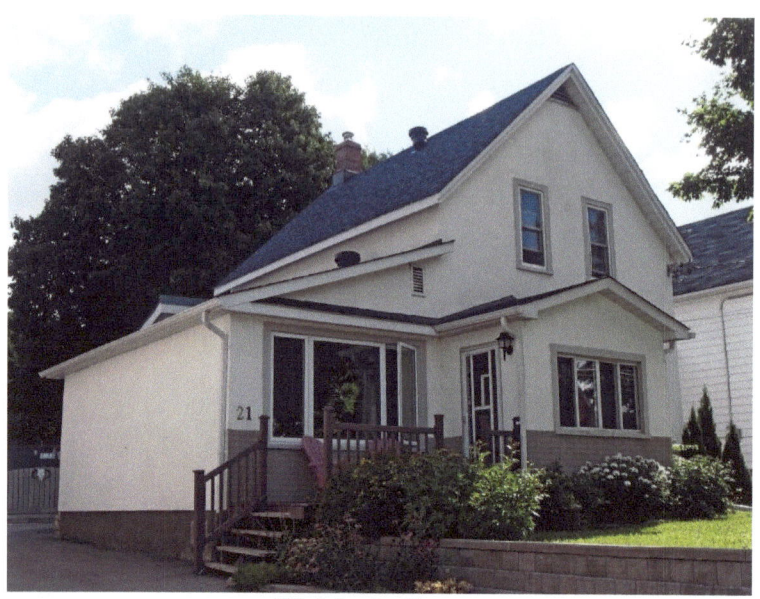

21 Maria Street

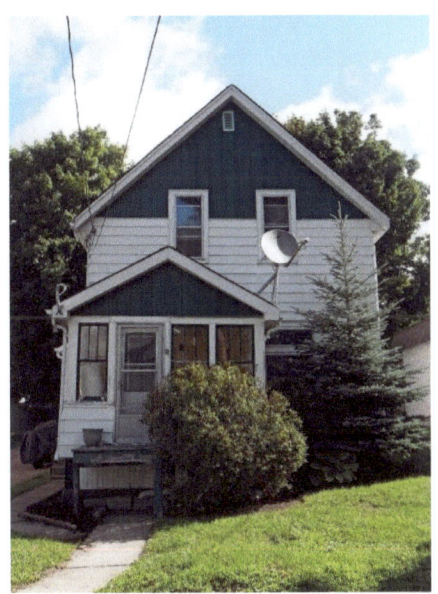

23 Maria Street – Gothic

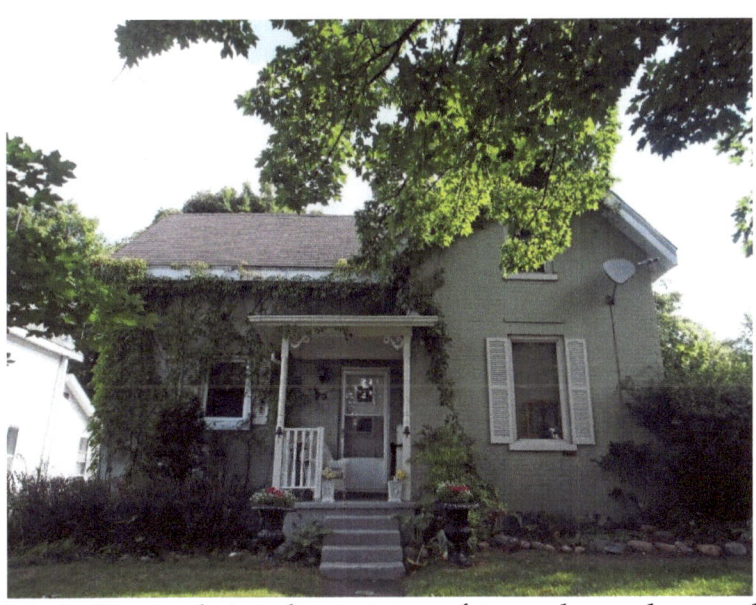

25 Maria Street - bric-a-brac at top of turned wood verandah
supports, open railing

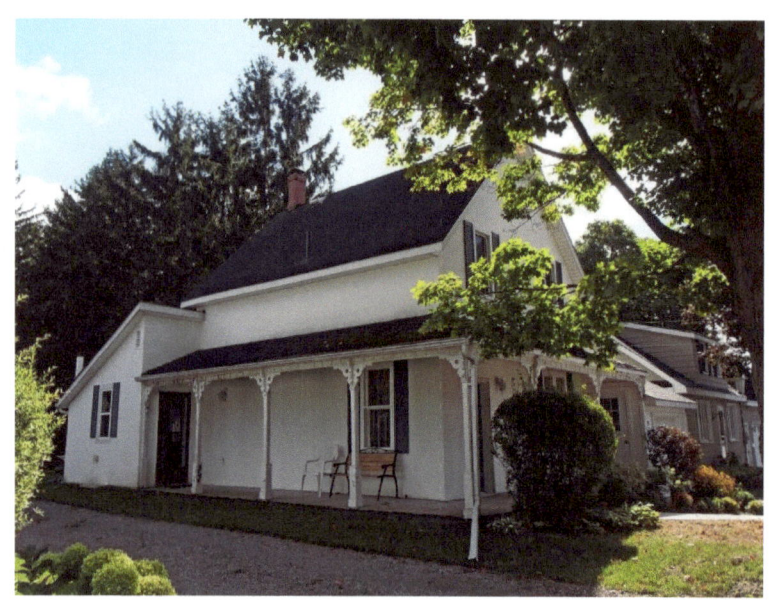

29 Maria Street – Gothic - bric-a-brac at top of wraparound verandah supports

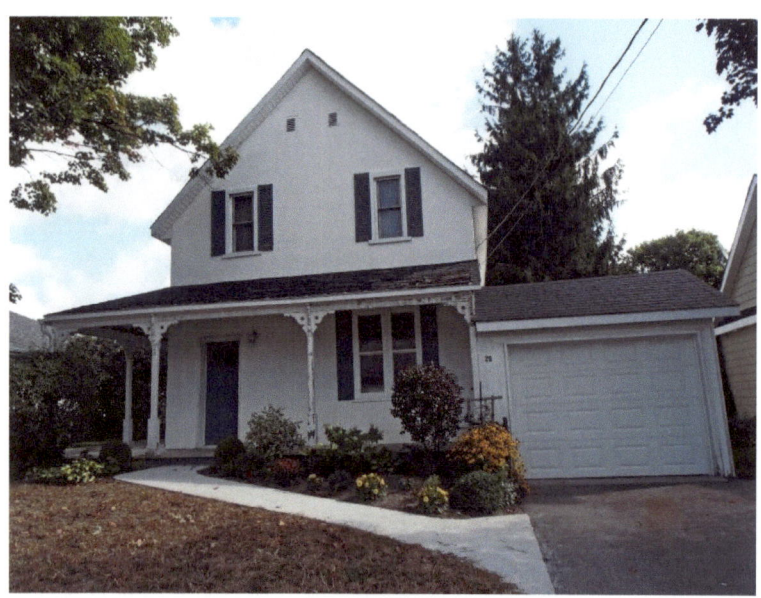

Gothic

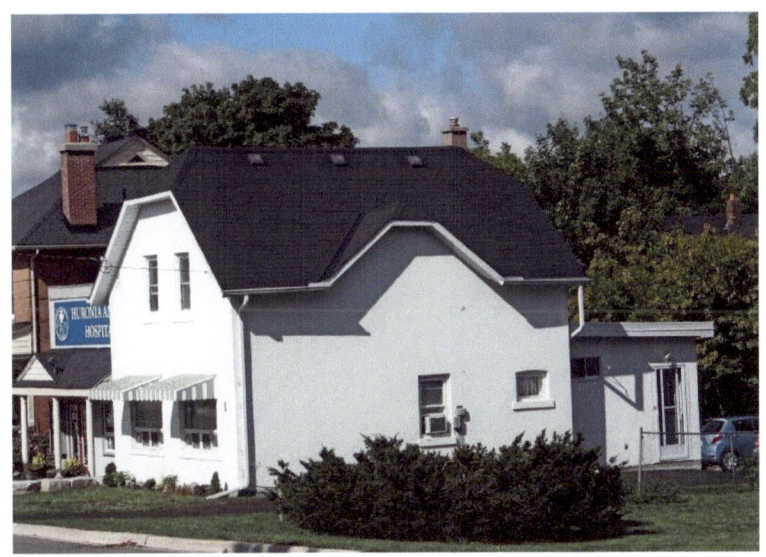

1 Maria Street

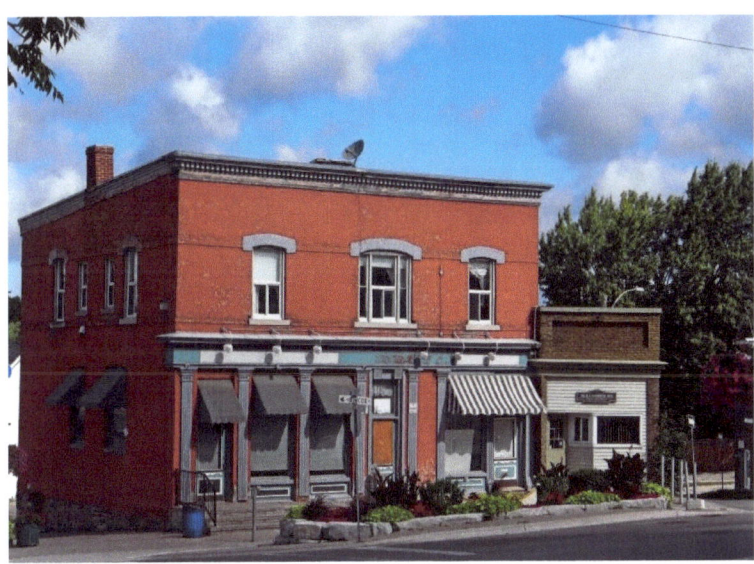

1-3 Simcoe Street – 1880s – flat roof, dentil moulding, voussoirs, pilasters

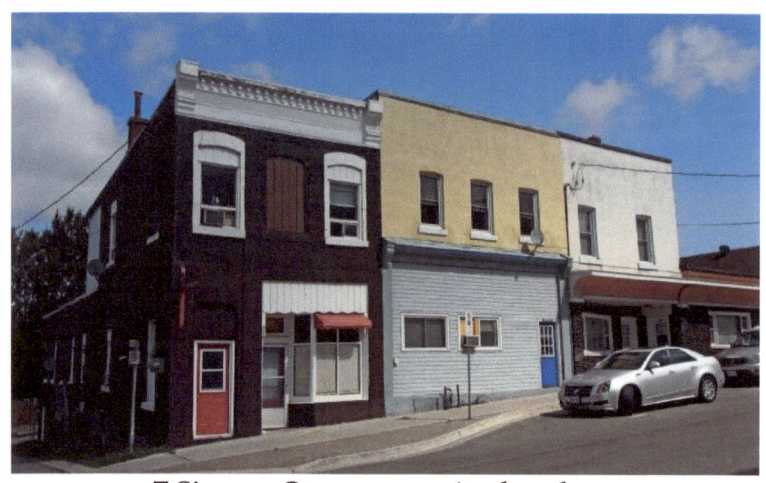

7 Simcoe Street – cornice brackets

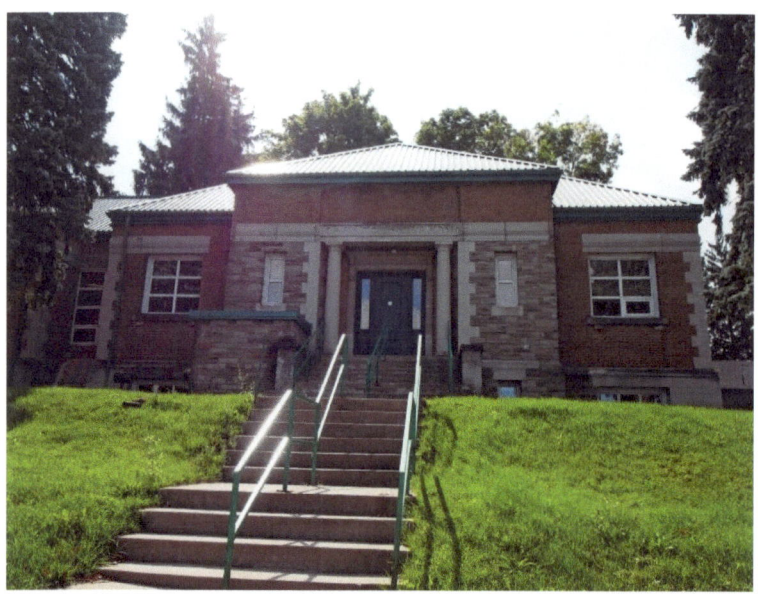

24 Simcoe Street – Carnegie Library – Andrew Carnegie, steel
industrialist, provided funds for the library on the condition
that the town provide a site centrally located and that they
pay at least ten per cent each year, of what Carnegie donated,
for maintenance of the building – built 1909-1910 – Doric
pillars, quoins - Arts and Crafts style with stone and brick

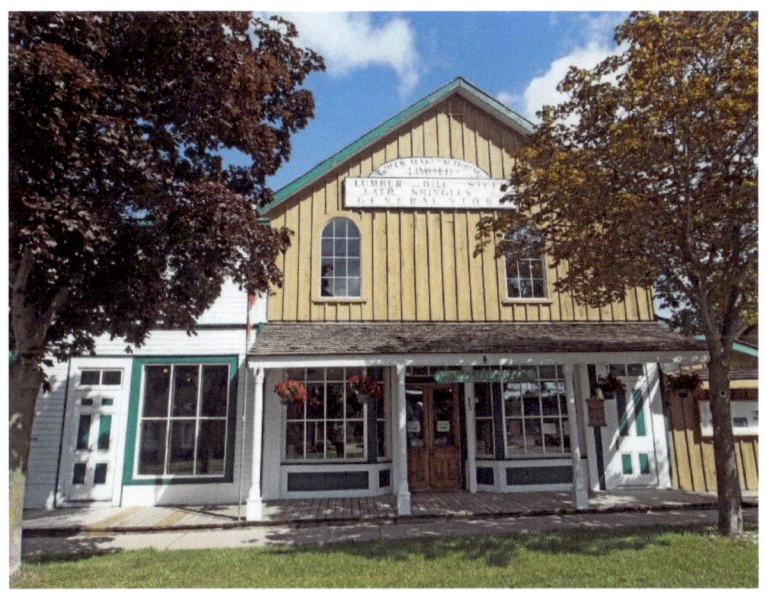

13 Burke Street – Penetanguishene Centennial Museum and Archives –
Charles Beck came here in 1865, operated an existing saw mill, and in 1873
built a larger saw mill called the "Red Mill"; in 1875 he built a general store
on Burke Street at the foot of Nelson; in 1968 Charles' great-grandson
donated the store to the town to become a museum

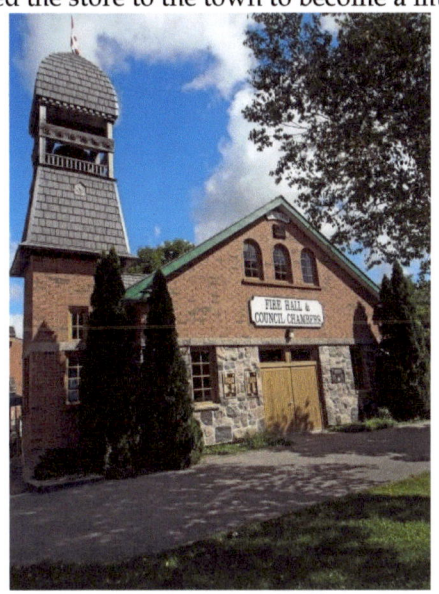

Replica Fire Hall

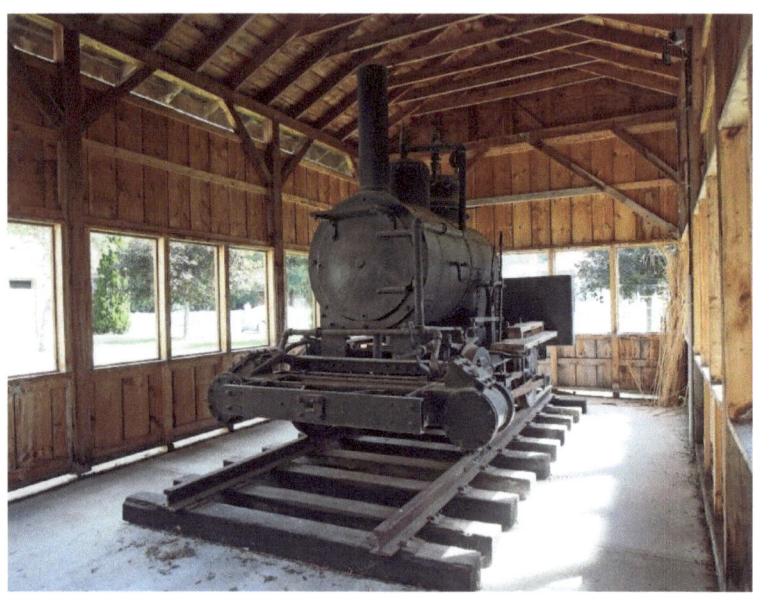

1879 Baldwin Steam Engine – served on the Hamilton Dundas Street Railway, a 15.4 kilometer interurban line between the two towns from 1878 to 1897; the engine was retired and bought by Charles Beck who used it as a yard switcher at his lumber mills

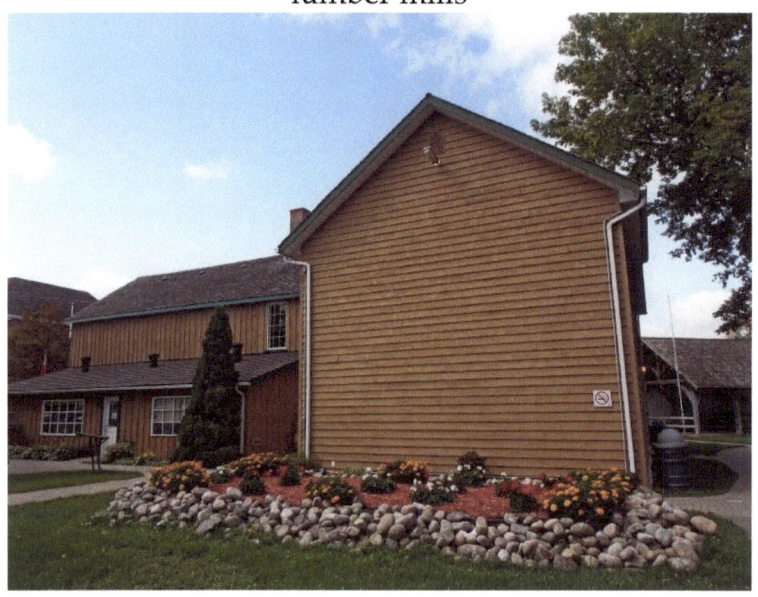

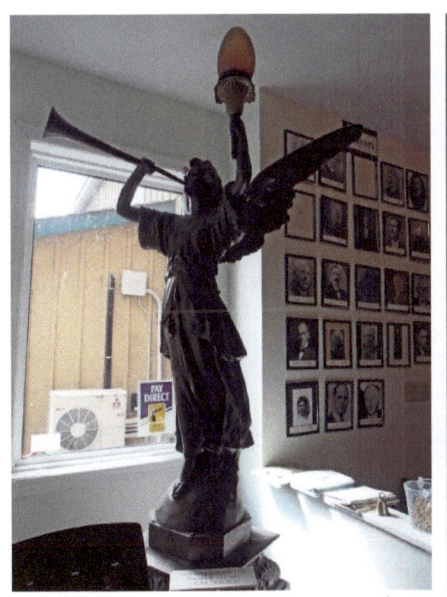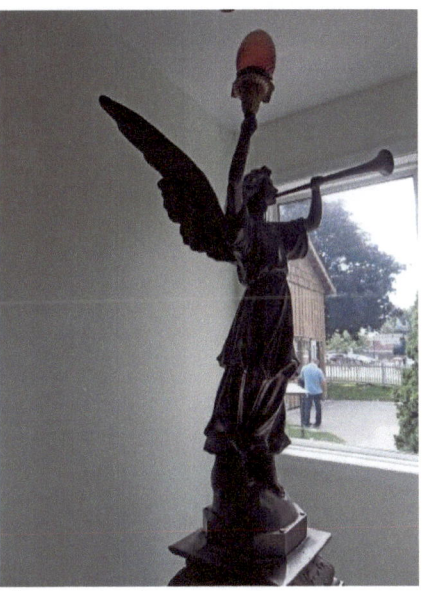

The two bronze statues of angels were given to the town to celebrate the 300th anniversary of Samuel de Champlain's landing at Toanche (Too on chee) across the bay from Penetanguishene. It symbolizes the good relations between the French and English.

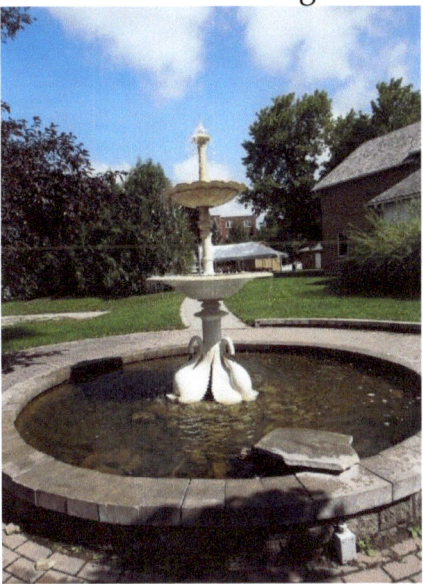

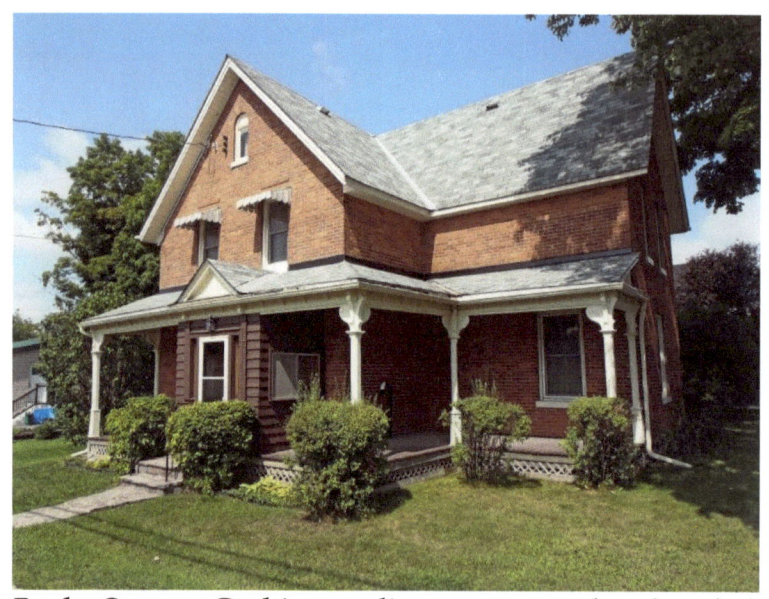

31 Burke Street – Gothic – pediment, cornice brackets below verandah roof

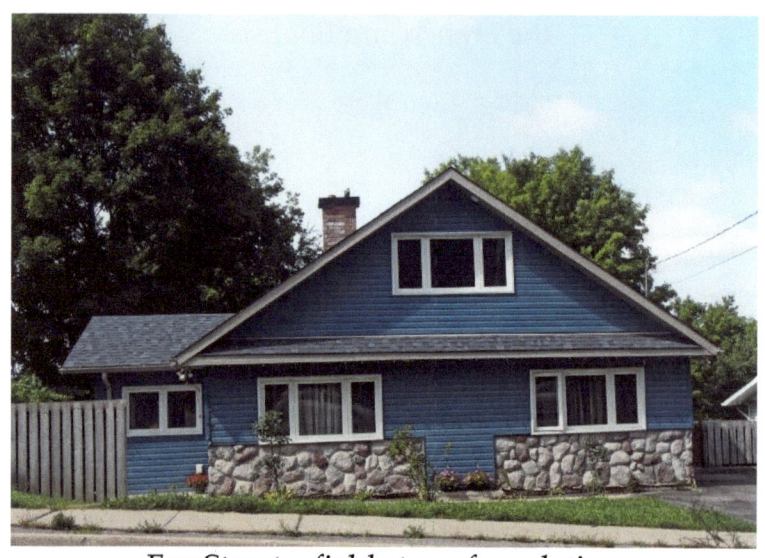

Fox Street – field stone foundation

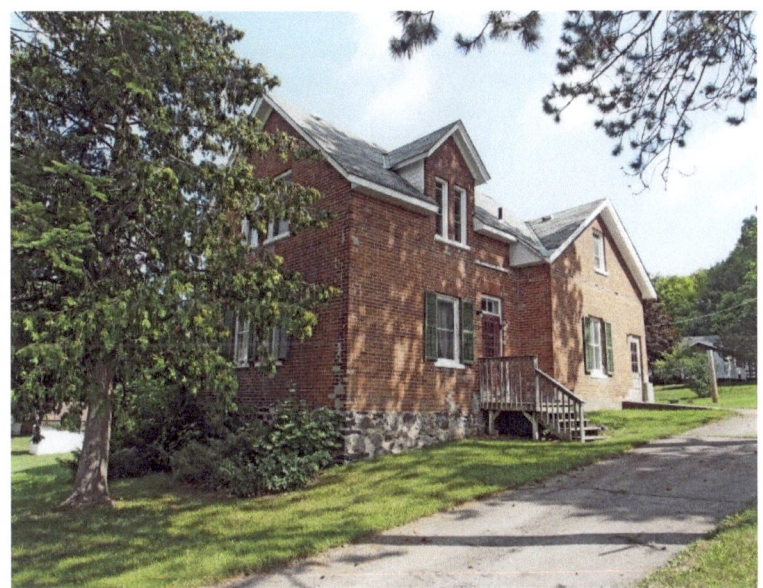

Fox Street – cobblestone foundation, dormer

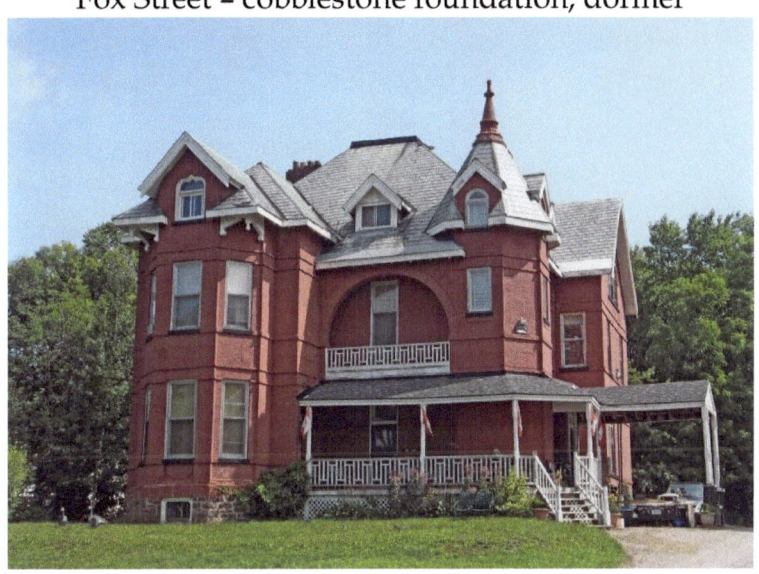

83 Fox Street – 1885 – home of Charles Beck and Amelia Dalms who had nine children (6 boys, 3 girls) – Queen Anne style – fretwork, turret, dormer, second-floor balcony, string courses wrap around the house; unique shape of window in gable

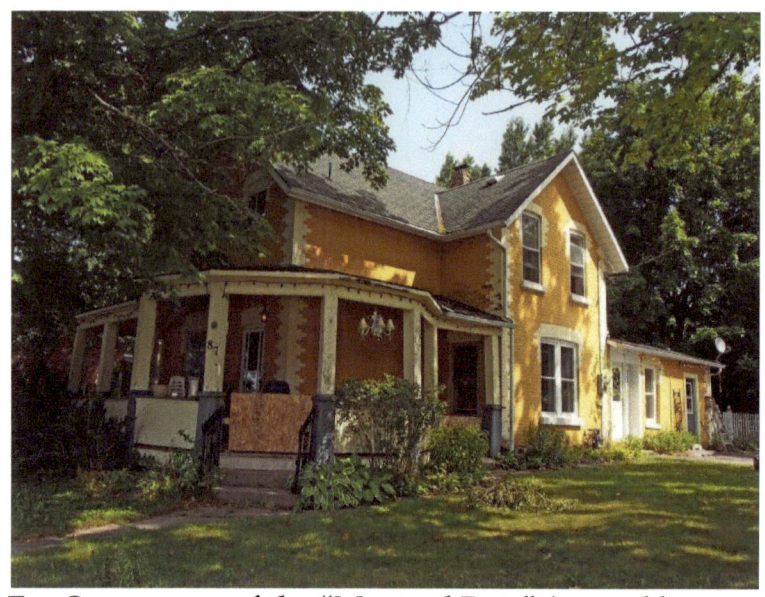

87 Fox Street – one of the "Mustard Pots" (named because of their colour) – owned by Charles Beck and rented to employees – Gothic, corner quoins, wraparound veranda

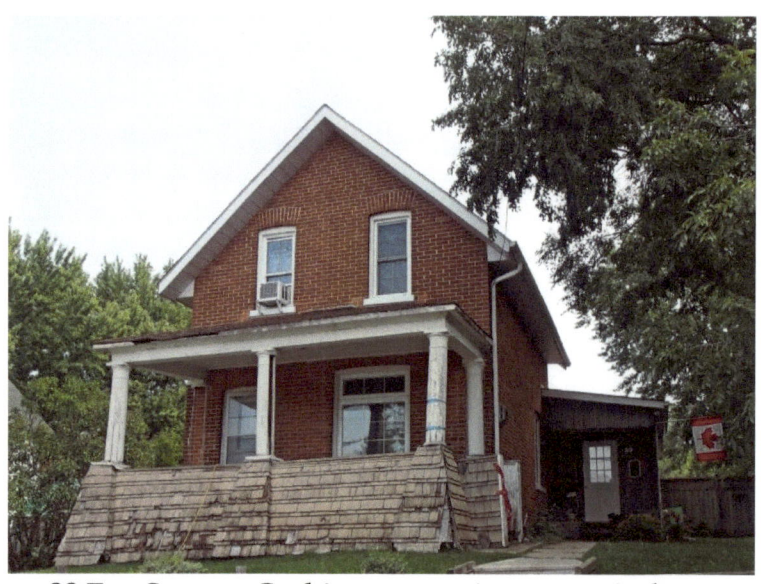

89 Fox Street – Gothic – voussoirs over windows

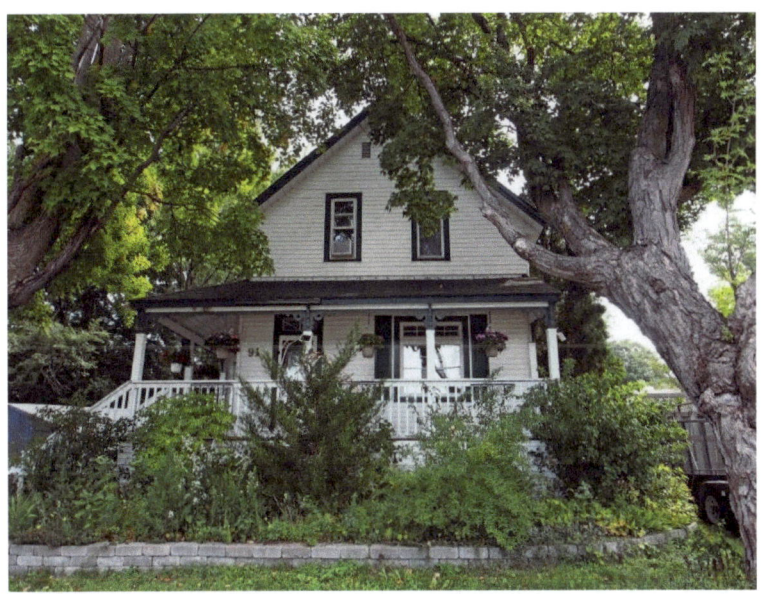

91 Fox Street – Gothic - bric-a-brac at top of verandah supports, open railing

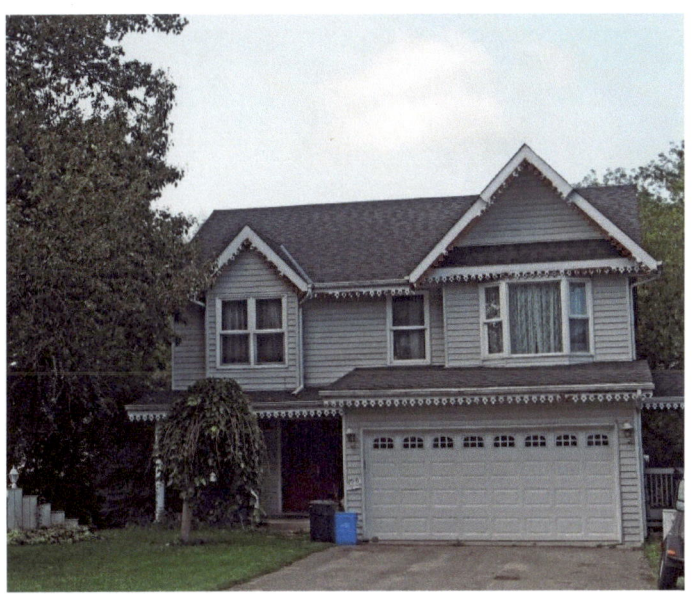

Verge board trim on gables and on cornice of veranda and garage

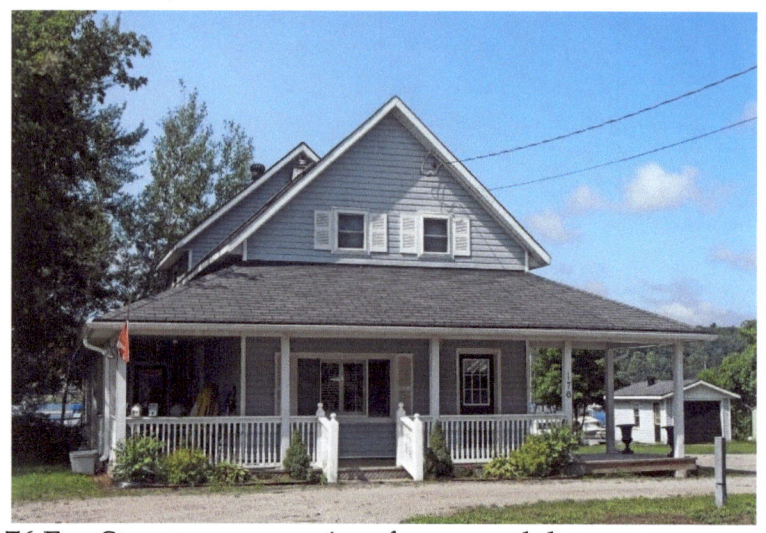

176 Fox Street – square piers for verandah supports, open railing

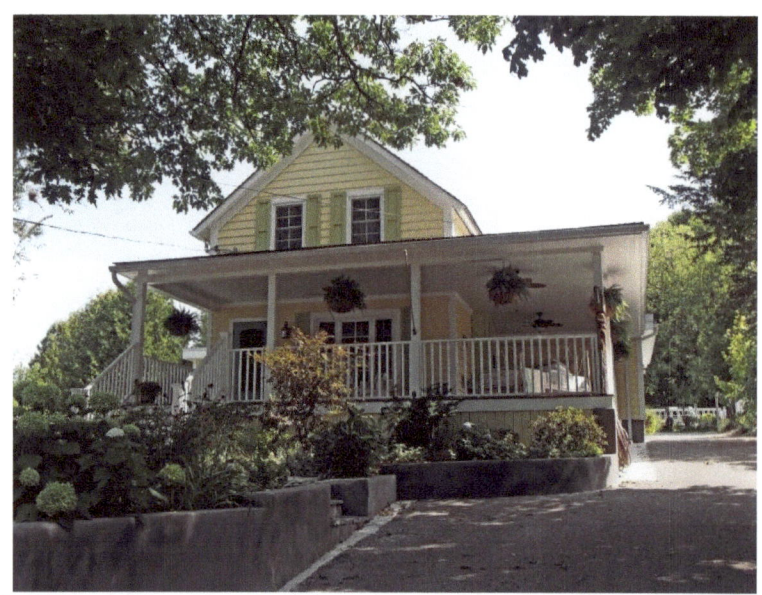

243 Church Street – Gothic – deep wraparound veranda with square piers and open railing

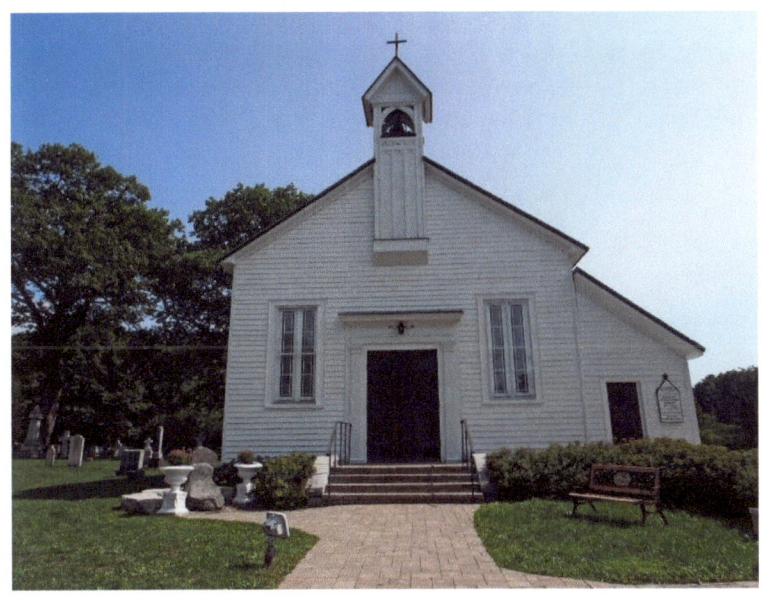

St. James-on-the-Lines Church - a small wooden Anglican church built 1836-1838 to serve the military garrison and civilian population

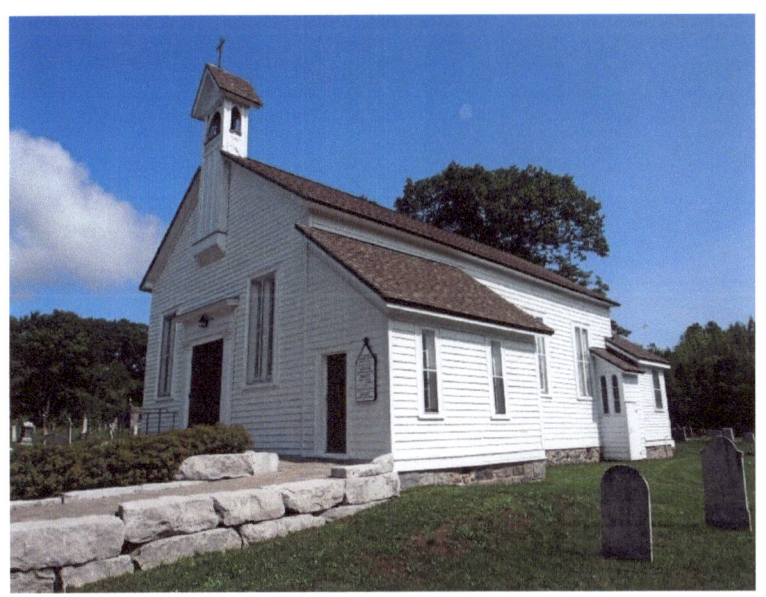

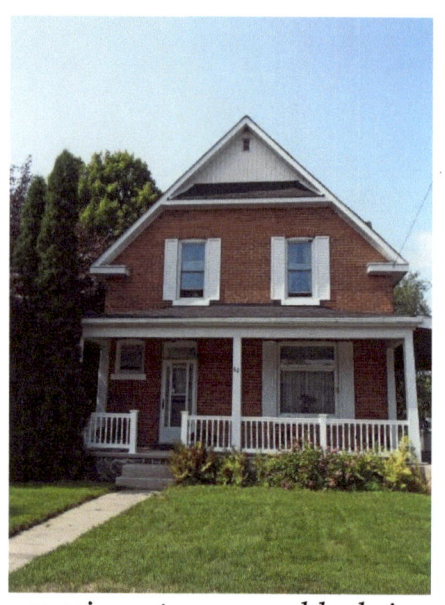

60 Peel Street – cornice return on gable; bric-a-brac at top of verandah supports, open railing

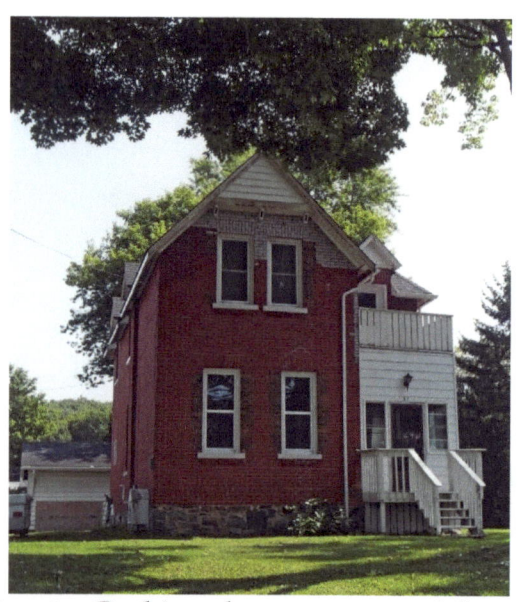

51 Peel Street – Gothic – dormers, second floor balcony, cobblestone foundation

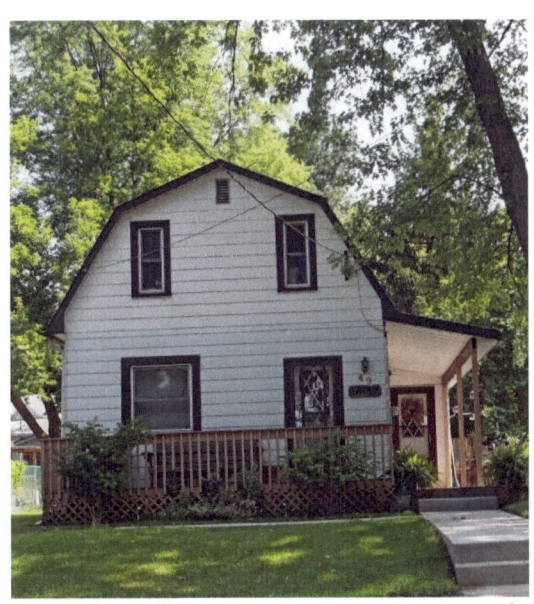

49 Peel Street – Neo-colonial style - gambrel roof; open railing

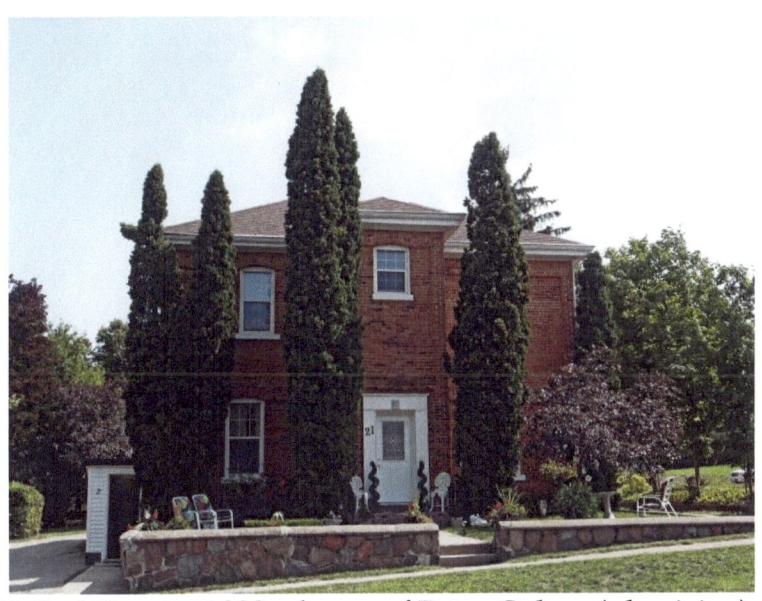

21 Peel Street – 1882 – home of Peter Gahau (physician) – hipped roof

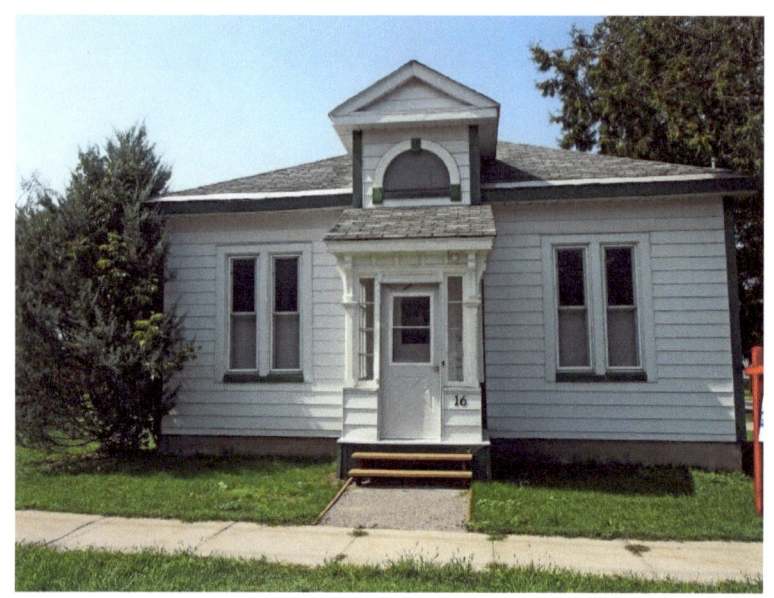

16 Peel Street – sidelights; pediment above dormer with keystone

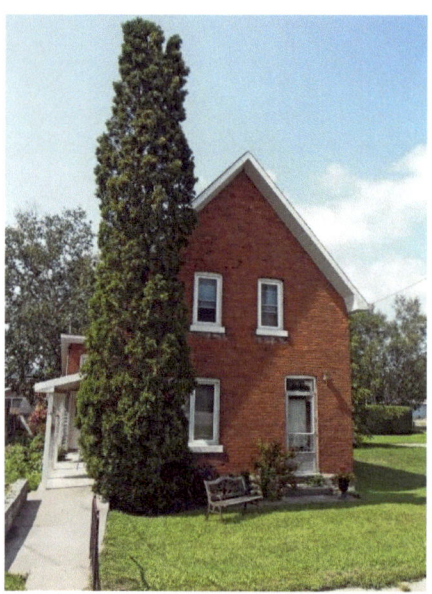

Gothic - gable

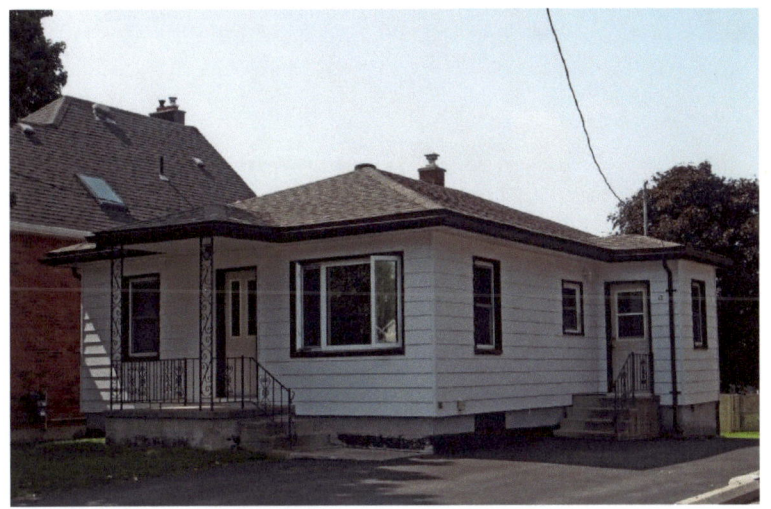

12 Peel Street – hipped roof

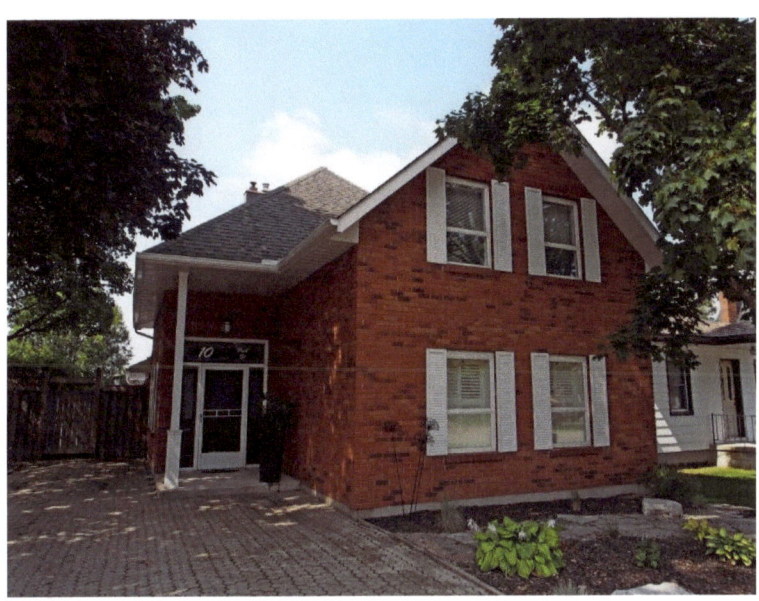

10 Peel Street - Gothic

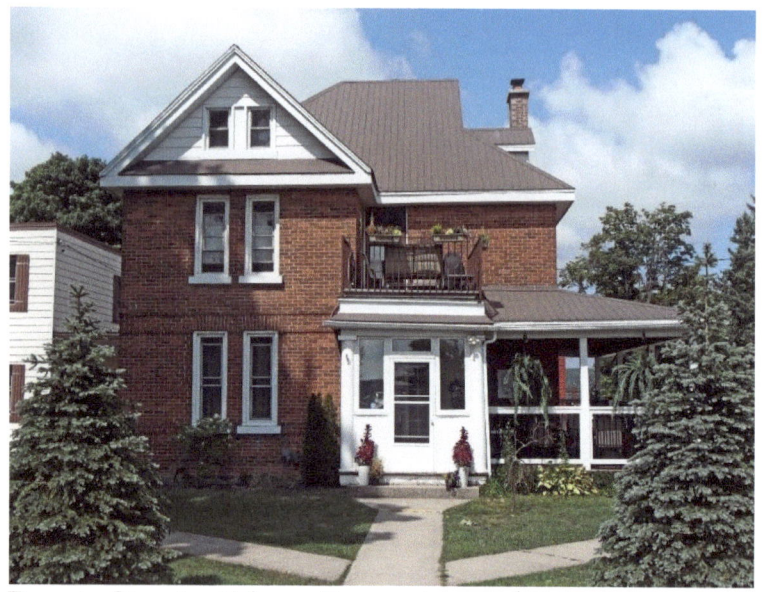

Poyntz Street – Edwardian – string courses around the building, second floor balcony

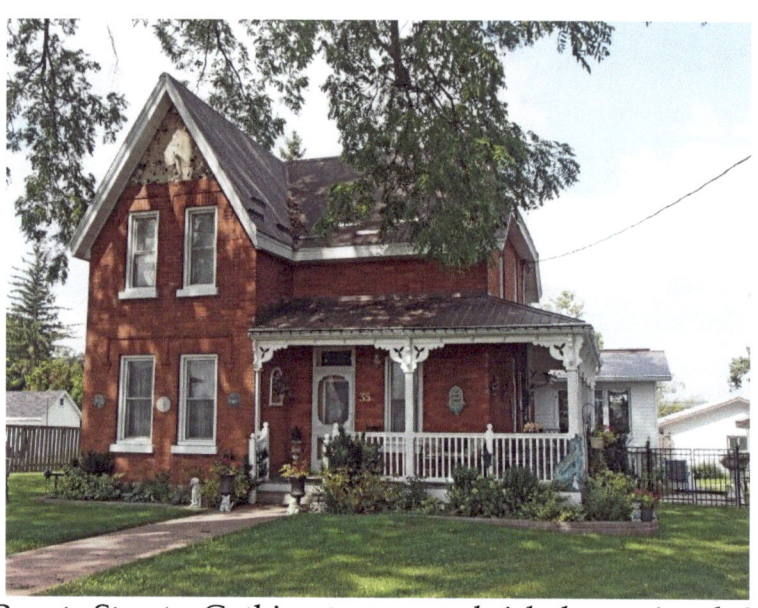

35 Poyntz Street – Gothic – terra cotta brick decoration; bric-a-brac at top of verandah supports, open railing

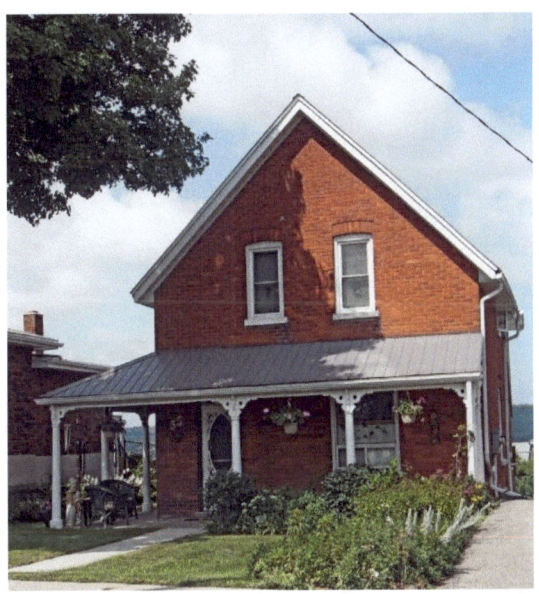

55 Poyntz Street – Gothic - bric-a-brac at top of verandah supports

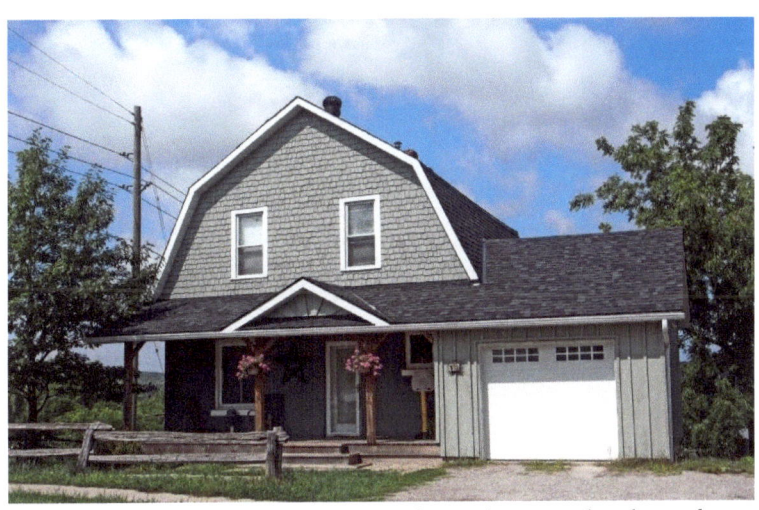

59 Poyntz Street – Neo-colonial – gambrel roof

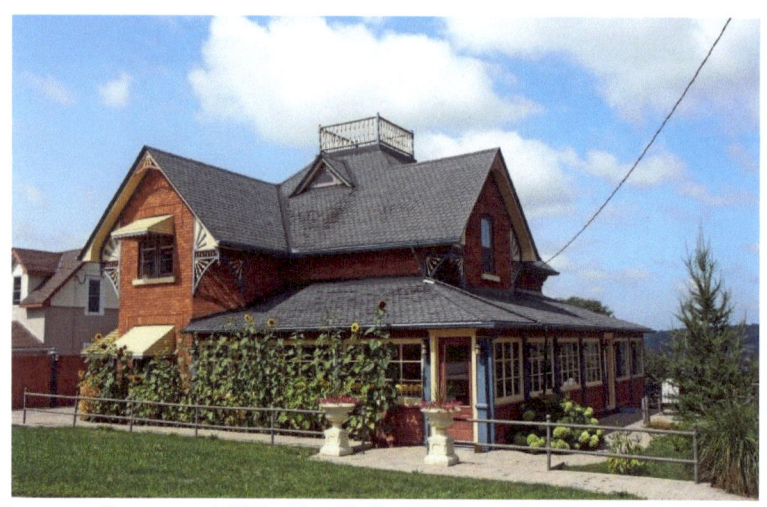

69 Poyntz Street – 1905 – built by George Pelletier, a carpenter; rooftop balcony above dormer; fretwork; enclosed wraparound veranda

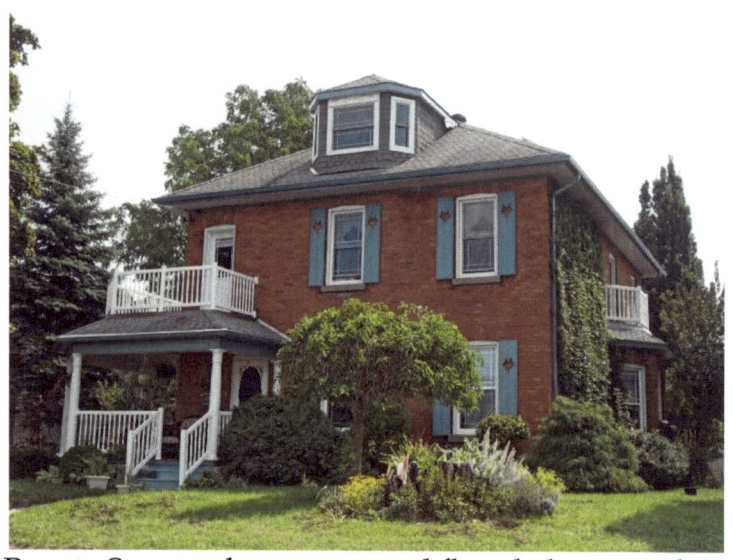

68 Poyntz Street – dormer, second floor balcony with open railing, porch with open railing; balcony above bay window on side

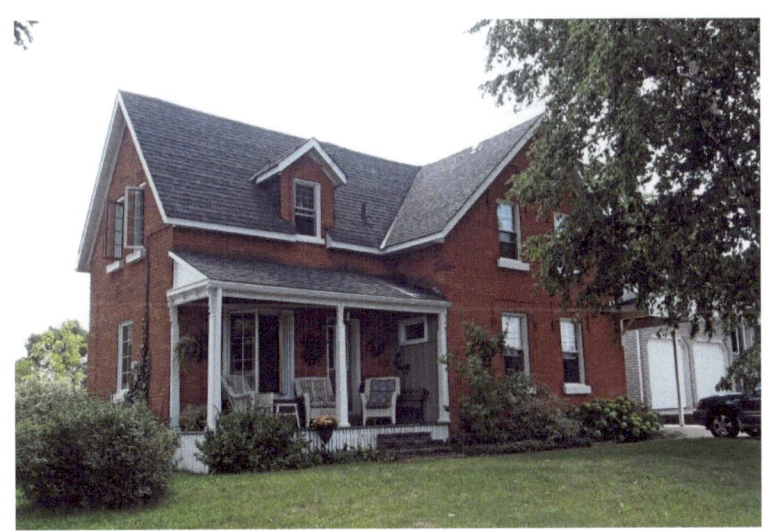

Poyntz Street – Gothic - dormer

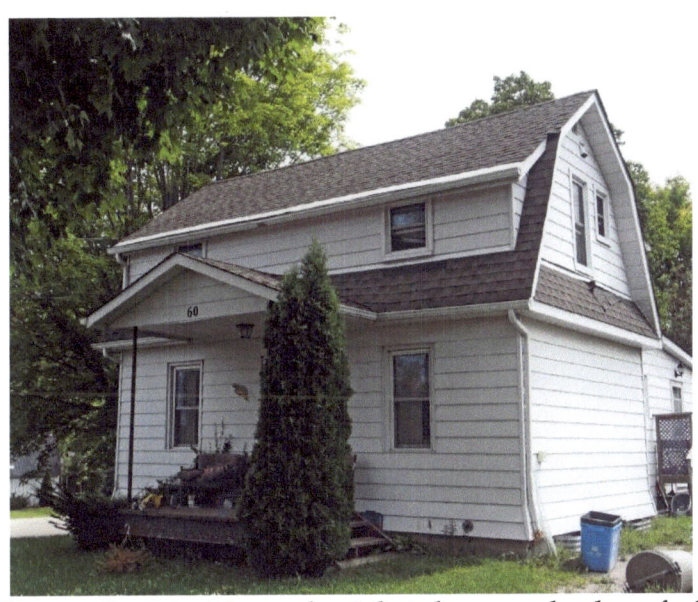

60 Poyntz Street – Neo-colonial style – gambrel roof, shed
dormer, pediment

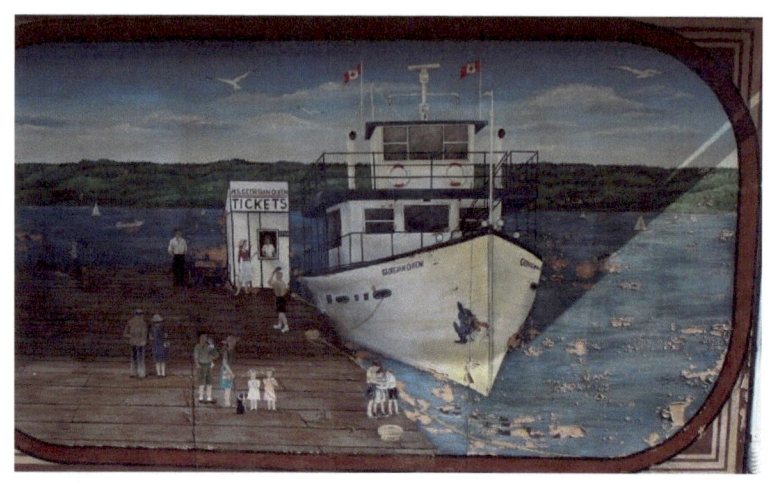

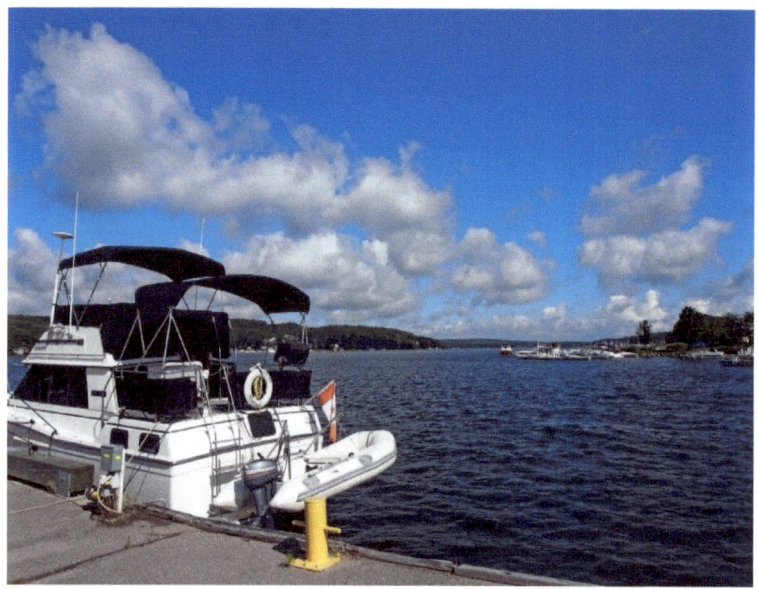

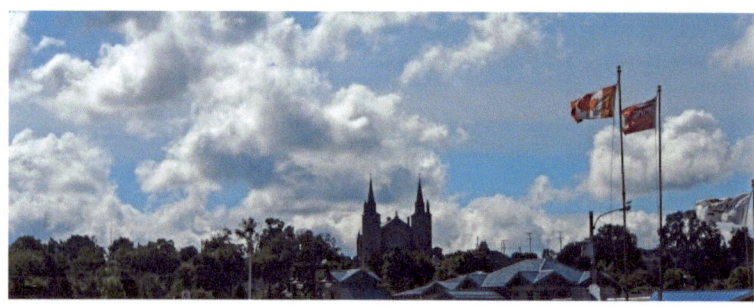

Discovery Harbour

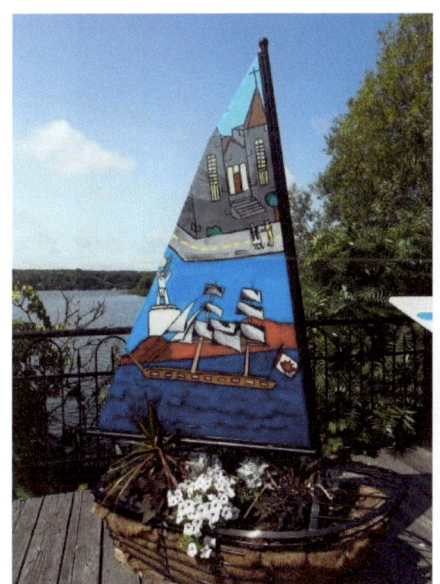 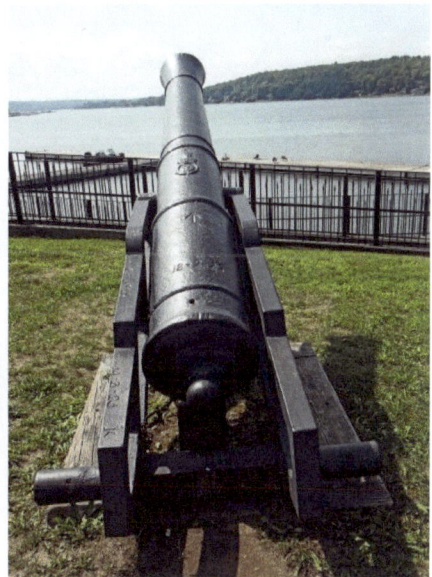

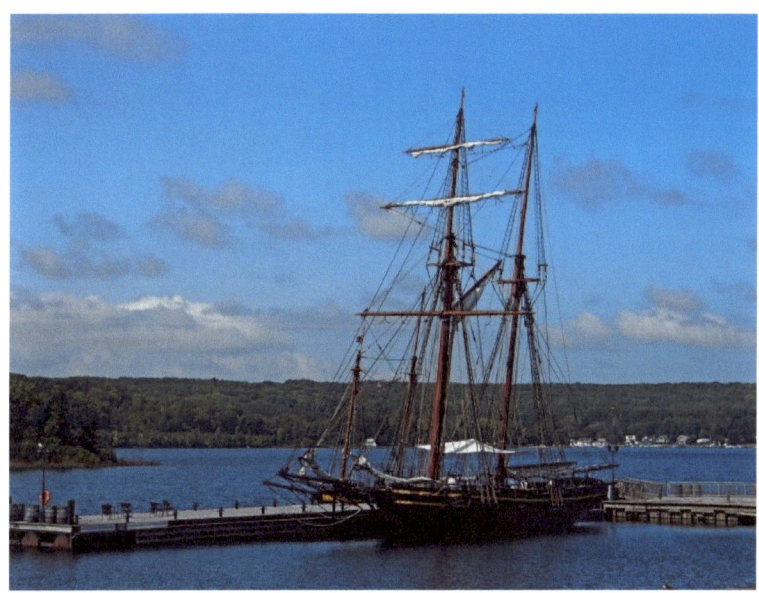

H.M.S. Tecumseh

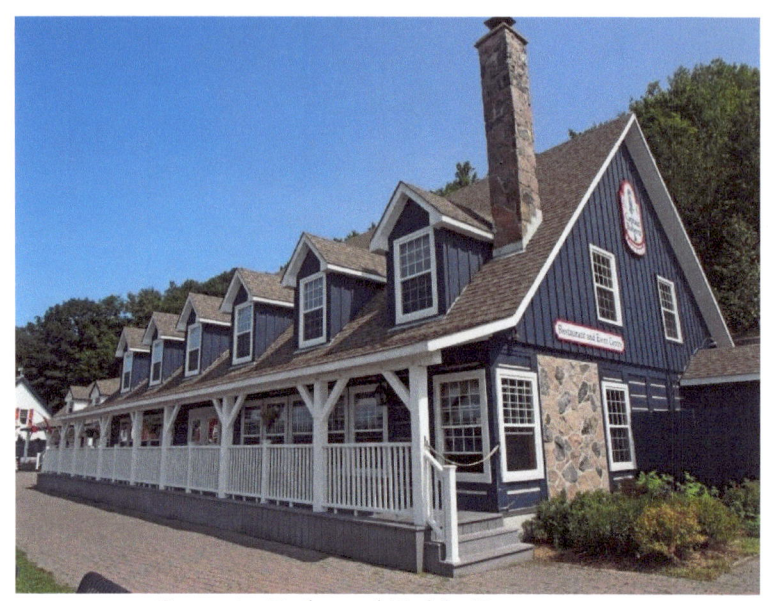

Captain Roberts' Table Restaurant

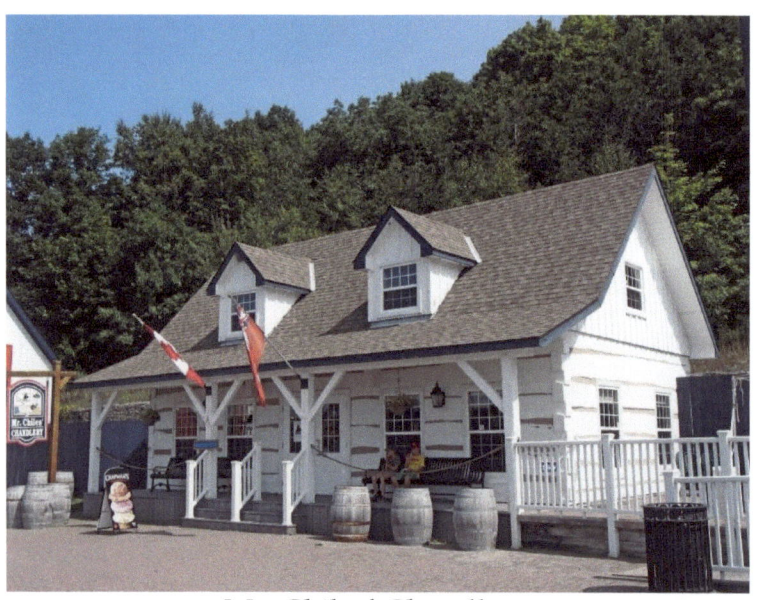

Mr. Chiles' Chandlery

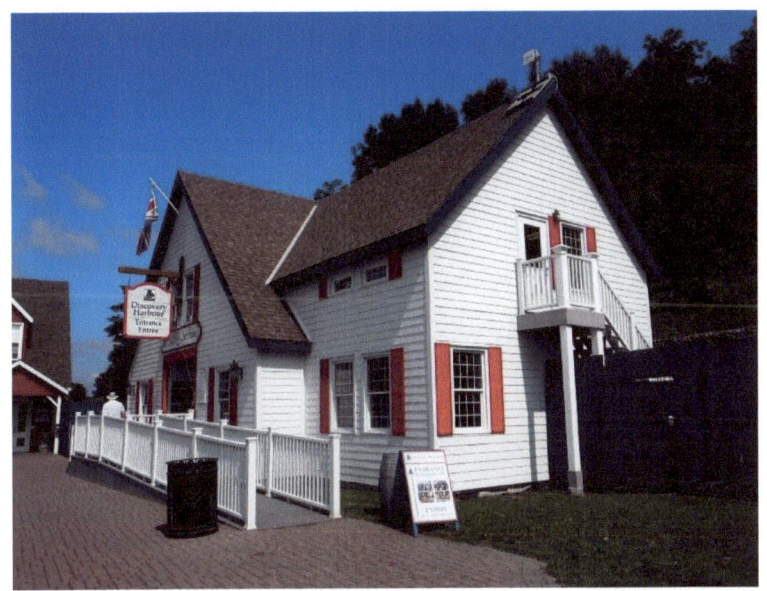

Bayfield's Charthouse and Visitor Centre

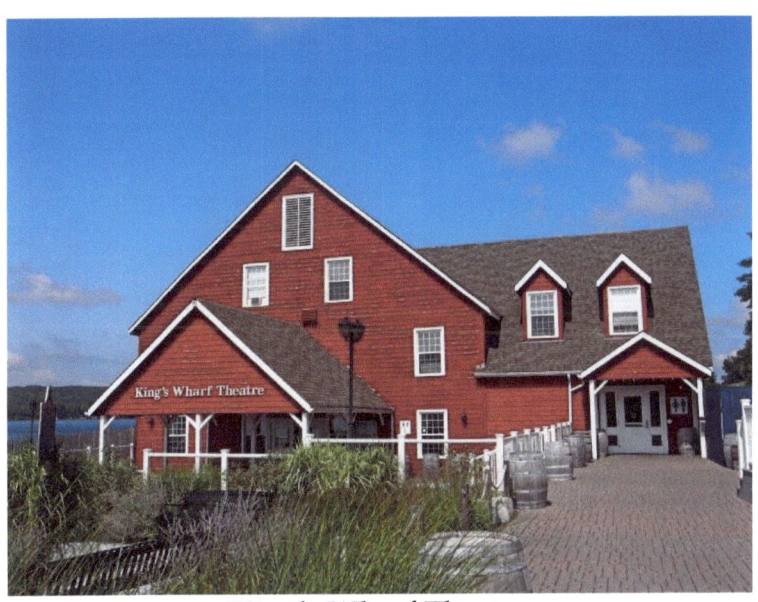

King's Wharf Theatre

Architectural Terms

Bay Window: A window that projects out from a wall, in a semicircular, rectangular, or polygonal design. Used frequently in Gothic and Victorian designs. Example: 3 Maria Street, Page 32	
Belvedere: (from the Italian "beautiful view") an architectural feature on a roof, in a garden or on a terrace that gives a beautiful view. Example: 33 Robert Street, Page 8	
Brackets: a decorative or weight-bearing structural element which forms a right angle with one side against a wall and the other under a projecting surface such as an eave or roof. Example: 78 Main Street, Page 18	
Buttress: a masonry structure built against or projecting from a wall which serves to support or reinforce the wall. In Canadian architecture, they are sometimes used for decoration. Example: 20 Robert Street, Page 9	
Capital: The uppermost finish or decoration on a column. An Ionic column has a small base, a thin elegant shaft, and a capital composed of volutes which are carved whirls or twists that take the form of a scroll. Example: 33 Robert Street, Page 8 A Doric column is characterized by a plain column with no base, a shaft with twenty flutings, and a simple capital with a simple entablature. Example: 131 Main Street, Page 33	 Ionic Doric

Cobblestone architecture: Refers to the use of cobblestones embedded in mortar as a method for erecting walls on houses and commercial buildings. Example: 33 Robert Street, Page 8	
Cornice Return: decorative element on the end of a gable. Example: 60 Peel Street, Page 51	
Course: continuous horizontal row or layer of stone or brick. Example: 83 Fox Street, Page 46	
Cupola: A domed or curved roof rising from a building as a decorative element. Example: 20 Robert Street, Page 9	
Dentil Moulding: an even series of rectangles used as ornamental decoration in cornices. Example: 73 Main Street, Page 18	
Dichromatic brickwork: the use of two colours of brick, tile or slate to decorate a façade. Example: 89 Main Street, Page 21	
Dormer: (French for "sleep") a gable end window that pierces through the plane of a sloping roof surface to create usable space in the top floor or attic of a building by adding headroom. Example: 12 Water Street, Page 16	

Fretwork: interlaced decorative design resembling a bracket Example: 69 Poyntz Street, Page 57	
Gable: the triangular portion of a wall between the edges of a sloping roof. **Jacobean Gable:** the gable extends above the roofline. Example: 28 Robert Street West, Page 7	
Gambrel Roof: a symmetrical two-sided roof with two slopes on each side; the upper slope is positioned at a shallow angle, while the lower slope is steep. It is similar to a mansard roof, but a gambrel has vertical gable ends instead of being hipped at the four corners of the building. Example: 143 Main Street, Page 25	
Hipped Roof: a roof where all sides slope downwards to the walls with no gables. Example: 131 Main Street, Page 23	
Keystones and Voussoirs: a voussoir is a wedge-shaped element used in building an arch. A keystone is the central stone that locks all the stones into position, allowing the arch to bear weight. A keystone is often enlarged and embellished. Example: 1 Water Street, Page 17	
Lancet Window: a tall, narrow window with a pointed arch at its top. Example: 20 Robert Street, Page 9	

Pediment: a triangular section above the door or portico, usually supported by columns. The inside of the triangle is called the tympanum. Example: 33 Robert Street, Page 8	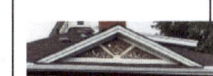
Quoin: masonry blocks at the corner of a wall, often a decorative feature, usually larger or of a different colour than the rest of the wall. Example: 18 Maria Street, Page 37	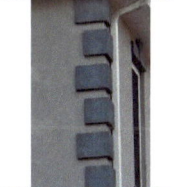
Rose Window: a circular window with ornamental tracery radiating from the centre. Example: 20 Robert Street, Page 9	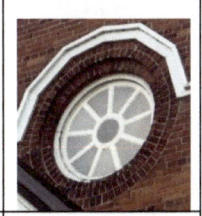
Sidelight: a vertical window that flanks a door, and is often used to emphasize the importance of a primary entrance. **Transom Window:** the light above the doorway, also called a fanlight. Example: 14 Water Street, Page 15	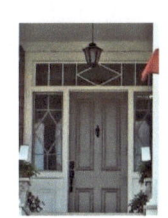
Turret: a small tower that projects from the wall of a building. Example: 18 Robert Street, Page 9	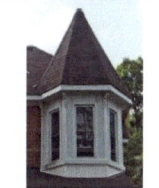
Verge board and Finial: also called bargeboards – hang from the projecting end of a roof and are often elaborately carved and ornamented. **Finial:** ornament added to the top of a gable, pinnacle, canopy or spire – a Gothic element. Example: 3 Maria Street, Page 32	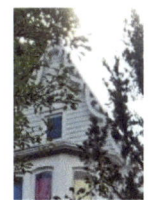

Arts and Crafts: The overlying theme - the house was based on the function of the house. Rooms were oriented to take advantage of the movement of the sun for warmth and light during daylight hours. Side entrances allowed for useable space on the front facade for light or garden use. Arts and Crafts houses have many of these features: wood, stone or stucco siding; low-pitched roof; wide eaves with triangular brackets; exposed roof rafters; porch with thick square or round columns; stone porch supports; exterior chimney made with stone; open floor plans with few hallways; many windows, some with stained or leaded glass; beamed ceilings; dark wood wainscoting and moldings; built-in cabinets, shelves, and seating. Example: 24 Simcoe Street, Page 42	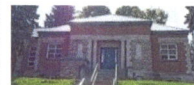
Edwardian, 1900-1930 – This style bridges the ornate and elaborate styles of the Victorian era and the simplified styles of the 20th century. Balanced facades, simple roof lines, dormer windows, large front porches, and smooth brick surfaces are its characteristics. Example: Poyntz Street, Page 55	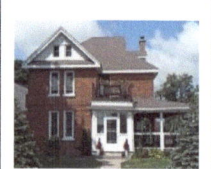
Gothic Revival, 1830-1890 – These decorative buildings have sharply-pitched gables with highly detailed verge boards, pointed-arch window openings, and dichromatic brickwork. It is a common style in Ontario. Example: 3 Maria Street, Page 32	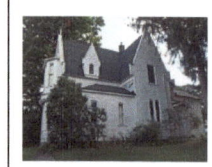

Neo-colonial (also Colonial Revival, Georgian Revival or Neo-Georgian) architecture seeks to revive elements of architectural style of American colonial architecture of the period around the Revolutionary War which drew strongly from Georgian architecture of Great Britain. Architecture from the 18th and early 19th centuries in Ontario includes a wide assortment of detailing and ornament applied to a design centered around the fireplace and the source of water. Structures are typically two stories, have a symmetrical front facade with elaborate front doorways, often with decorative crown pediments, fanlights, and sidelights, symmetrical windows flanking the front entrance, often in pairs or threes, and columned porches. Example: 143 Main Street, Page 25	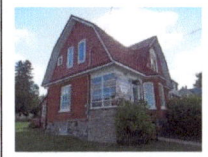
Queen Anne, 1885-1900 – This style is distinguished by an irregular outline featuring a combination of an offset tower, broad gables, projecting two-storey bays, verandahs, multi-sloped roofs, and tall, decorative chimneys. A mixture of brick and wood is common. Windows often have one large single-paned bottom sash and small panes in the upper sash. Example: 83 Fox Street, Page 46	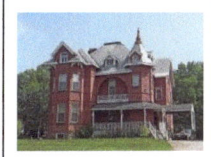

Romanesque Revival, 1880-1910 – This style hearkens back to medieval architecture of the 11th and 12th centuries with a heavy appearance, blocky towers and rounded arches. Example: 28 Robert Street West, Page 7	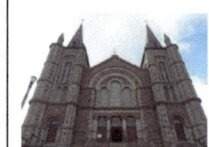
Saltbox: A saltbox is a building with a long, pitched roof that slopes down to the back, generally a wooden frame house. A saltbox has just one storey in the back and two stories in the front. The asymmetry of the unequal sides and the long, low rear roof line are the most distinctive features of a saltbox, which takes its name from its resemblance to a wooden lidded box in which salt was once kept. The earliest saltbox houses were created when a lean-to addition was added onto the rear of the original house extending the roof line sometimes to less than six feet from ground level. Example: 18 Harriet Street, Page 30	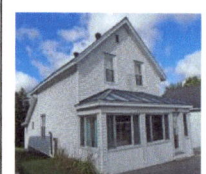

www.ingramcontent.com/pod-product-compliance
Lightning Source LLC
Chambersburg PA
CBHW040838180526
45159CB00001B/229